Tips On Grandparent Rights In California

TIPS ON GRANDPARENT RIGHTS IN CALIFORNIA

©1998 by E. F. CASH-DUDLEY

First Printing, September, 1998
Made in the United States of America

Cover Design by E. F. Cash-Dudley, Bill Dudley-Cash, Susan Shaw
Graphics by Western Graphics
Typeset by Tish Carter
Published by
E. F. Cash-Dudley, Esq.
A Professional Law Corporation
Publications Division
P.O. Box 3772
Burbank, CA 91508

ISBN#0-9665469-0-3

PREFACE

Some reports indicate that as many as seventy percent of all marriages will end in divorce. There is also a skyrocketing increase in the number of children born out-of-wedlock. This social phenomenon creates an uncertainty in grandparents about their role and legal rights. Many times, grandparents are not included in family decisions. Each year, more and more grandparents resort to the legal system to maintain contact with their grandchildren.

The purpose of this book is to provide insight into the legal rights of grandparents. The questionnaire in *chapter one* will allow you to determine as a grandparent whether or not you are eligible to file a petition for grandparent rights. *Chapters two, three, four,* and *five* describe the criteria and court processes for each type of grandparent action. *Chapter six* is an overview of the types of fees that are typical for different types of actions. *Chapter seven* is based on many years of experience as a Family Law Specialist managing custody and grandparent visitation cases. This chapter also includes tips on how to implement court orders and how to avoid the pitfalls of working with a former in-law. Sections of the pertinent laws are attached at the end of this book.

Each county has its own process for implementing grandparent rights. This book contains an overview of the current process plus information from each county. A helpful tip is to telephone your local county Superior Court Clerk's office for information specific to your case. Addresses and telephone numbers are located in the back of this book.

Any comments or questions? Please feel free to contact me via e-mail at cashdudley@aspaq.com or visit my website at www.aspaq.com. You can also write to me at 1608 F Street, Modesto, CA, 95354. To order additional copies, mail in the order form located in the back of the book.

As a grandmother myself, I hope you find this book extremely helpful.
GOOD LUCK!

E. F. Cash-Dudley, Esq.

TABLE OF CONTENTS

CHAPTER   PAGE

CHAPTER   PAGE

CHAPTER   PAGE

CHAPTER   PAGE

Chapter One

TYPES OF LEGAL ACTIONS

The following questionnaire will help guide you in determining whether you have the right to have a court action to exert grandparent rights and, if so, what type of court action you should file.

EXAMPLE

YES	NO	
		Are you a biological grandparent of the grandchild?

Although the statutes which refer to grandparents do not specifically state a biological grandparent, it is generally assumed that grandparent rights only apply to biological grandparents. Some judges will allow step-grandparents to participate in grandparent visitation cases, others will not.

The following examples <u>assume</u> no court actions regarding custody have been filed relating to this grandchild.

TABLE ONE

YES	NO	
		Are the mother and father married, living together and do both object to grandparent visitation?
		Does the grandchild live in the state of California?

If you have answered YES to both of the above questions, unfortunately, grandparents do not have a right to file a lawsuit for grandparent visitation.

TABLE TWO

YES	NO	
		Are the parents of the grandchild married?
		Does the grandchild live with someone other than the parents?
		Does the person who has custody object to your visitation?
		Does the grandchild live in California?

If you have answered YES to all of the above questions, go to Chapter Two, Independent Petition - Type One for more details. If you have answered NO to any of the above questions, proceed to Table Three.

TABLE THREE

YES	NO	
		Are the parents of the grandchild married?
		Is one of the parents missing and their whereabouts are unknown?
		Does the custodial parent object to your visitation?
		Does the grandchild live in California?

If you have answered YES to all of the above questions, go to Chapter Two, Independent Petition - Type One for more details. If you have answered NO to any of the above questions, proceed to Table Four.

TABLE FOUR

YES	NO	
		Are the parents of the grandchild married and living together?
		Does one of the parents object to your having time with the grandchild?
		Will the other parent join with you in the lawsuit?
		Does the grandchild live in California?

If you have answered YES to all of the above questions, go to Chapter Two, Independent Petition - Type One for more details. If you have answered NO to any of the above questions, please proceed to Table Five.

TABLE FIVE

YES	NO	
		Are the parents married but separated?
		Does the custodial parent object to your having time with the grandchild?
		Does the grandchild live in California?

If you have answered YES to all of the above questions, go to Chapter Two, Independent Petition - Type One for more details. If you have answered NO to any of the above questions, proceed to Table Six.

TABLE SIX

YES	NO	
		Is the grandchild living with you at this time with permission of the parent(s)?
		Is the agreement that the grandchild will continue to live with you?

If you have answered YES to both of the above questions, go to Chapter Three, Type One - Probate Court for more details. If you have answered NO to either of the above questions, proceed to Table Seven.

TABLE SEVEN

YES	NO	
		Is the grandchild living in a situation where you believe there exists a threat to the grandchild's safety and welfare?
		Are you willing to have the grandchild live with you?
		Does the grandchild live in California?

If you have answered YES to all of the above questions, go to Chapter Three, Type One - Probate Court for more details. If you have answered NO to any of the above questions, proceed to Table Eight.

TABLE EIGHT

YES	NO	
		Are you the mother or father of a deceased parent of the grandchild?
		Does the surviving parent prevent you from visiting the grandchild?
		Does the grandchild live in the state of California?

If you have answered YES to all of the above questions, go to Chapter Two, Independent Petition - Type Two for more details. If you have answered NO to any of the above questions, proceed to Table Nine.

The following questions assume that a court action relating to the grandchild has been filed by someone other than you.

TABLE NINE

YES	NO	
		Has the grandchild been adopted by someone not related to you?

There is no method available to obtain grandparent visitation under these circumstances.

TABLE TEN

YES	NO	
		Has the District Attorney Family Support Division filed for child support for the grandchild?

If a lawsuit has been filed by the District Attorney for child support, the grandparent cannot use this lawsuit to obtain visitation.

TABLE ELEVEN

YES	NO	
		Has one of the parents filed for any of the following? **-Dissolution of Marriage** **-Legal Separation** **-Nullity of Marriage** **-Complaint to Establish Paternity** **-Complaint to Establish Parental Relationship** **-Petition for Exclusive Custody of Child**
		Does the custodial parent prevent you from having visitations?
		Does the grandchild reside in California?

If you have answered YES to all of the above questions, go to Chapter Two, Joinder - Type Three for more details. If you have answered NO to any of the above questions, proceed to Table Twelve.

TABLE TWELVE

YES	NO	
		Does someone other than a parent have custody of the grandchild under a guardianship?
		Has the guardian objected to your visitation?
		Do the grandchild and guardian live in California?

If you have answered YES to all of the above questions, go to Chapter Three, Type One - Probate Court for more details. If you have answered NO to all of the above questions, proceed to Table Thirteen.

TABLE THIRTEEN

YES	NO	
		Does someone other than a parent have custody of the grandchild under a guardianship issued by the juvenile court?
		Has the guardian objected to your visitation?
		Do the grandchild and guardian live in California?

If you have answered YES to all of the above questions, go to Chapter Three, Type Two - Juvenile Court for more details. If you have answered NO to any of the above questions, proceed to Table Fourteen.

TABLE FOURTEEN

YES	NO	
		Has the grandchild been declared a dependent of the court by the Juvenile Court and placed with someone else?
		Has the person in charge of the grandchild objected to visitation?
		Does the grandchild live in California?

If you have answered YES to all of the above questions, go to Chapter Four, Juvenile Court - Dependency Actions for more details. If you have answered NO to any of the above questions, proceed to Table Fifteen.

TABLE FIFTEEN

YES	NO	
		Is your grandchild in the process of being adopted by a relative in an adoption case or being adopted by a relative through a Juvenile Court action?

If you have answered YES to the above question, go to Chapter Five, Type One - Kinship Adoptions for more details.

If none of the above questions apply to your individual situation, contact a Family Law Specialist for a consultation.

Chapter Two

FAMILY LAW COURT CASES

Custody and visitation with children are based on the philosophy that it is in the best interests of children to have contact with extended family members.

INDEPENDENT PETITION - TYPE ONE

One method of obtaining time with a grandchild is through Family Code 3104 which expands grandparent visitation rights under a specific set of circumstances. These circumstances are listed in the statute as set forth below and establish a fact pattern for grandparent rights.

If the parents meet one of the following criteria, the court has authority to order grandparent visitation:

      (1)   parents are separated and living apart; or
      (2)   one parent is absent and his or her whereabouts is unknown; or
      (3)   one parent joins in the grandparents' petition; or
      (4)   the child does not live with either parent.

Visitation is not automatic or guaranteed. To allow visitation, the court must make a finding that:

      (1)   visitation is in the child's best interest;
      (2)   there must be a pre-existing bond between the child and the grandparents that justifies visitation and;
      (3)   the child's interest in visitation must outweigh the parents' rights to exercise parental authority.

If the condition that was used to make the visitation order no longer exists, the court must terminate its order for grandparent visitation.

If the parents are married and living together and one parent has prevented the visitation of the grandchild with a grandparent, the grandparent with the cooperation of the other parent may petition for visitation. What this means is one of the parents still in the marriage, along with his or her parent(s), asks the court to allow the child to visit that grandparent(s). There is no clue given as to what this would do to the marriage when one parent participates in a lawsuit against the other parent with whom they are residing. This lawsuit is rarely used. The underlying assumption is that if the mother and father are living together, then each parent is making sure the grandchild has contact with the respective grandparents.

INDEPENDENT PETITION - TYPE TWO

The second method of obtaining time with a grandchild is where the grandparent files a petition for visitation when the grandparents' child (a parent) dies. The person who died was a biological parent of the child with whom the visitation is being sought. This statute is not limited to grandparents, but extends to siblings, great-grandparents, or other children of the decedent.

Where to File the Petition - Jurisdiction

The court of jurisdiction over custody and visitation is the Superior Court in the state where the child has lived for the past six months. The lawsuit is also to be brought in the county where the child lives. There are "emergency" exceptions to this rule which will allow the lawsuit to be brought in the county where the child currently lives even though the child may not have lived there for six months. A family law attorney can advise on the issue of jurisdiction if there is a question that arises regarding where to file the action.

Mediation Process

After either of the independent petitions are filed, a court date is requested to arrive at a visitation arrangement. Both cases are required to go through the mediation process. A detailed step-by-step process follows the information found in the Joinder section.

JOINDER - TYPE THREE

This is the MOST common legal method of obtaining time with your grandchild. A legal action already exists. The underlying lawsuit which is joined may be a Dissolution of Marriage, Legal Separation, Annulment, Action To Establish Paternity, Action To Establish Parental Relationship or Action To Establish Custody And Visitation and must be between the biological parents. The process by which grandparents obtain visitation for themselves is through a joinder action. Joinder means that the grandparent actually becomes a party in the existing or underlying action just like mom and dad.

A grandparent cannot be joined to an action brought by the District Attorney's Family Support Division to collect child support. If the District Attorney's Child Support Division has already established paternity, then either parent can file a Complaint to Establish Parental Relationship to raise the issues of custody and visitation.

The request for joinder is set in the Family Law Department. In some counties, this is referred to as the Domestic Relations Department. At the same time, there should be a request filed for a court date to participate in mediation.

Although technically the grandparents must be joined before they can participate in mediation, these matters may be taken care of on the same date. This depends on the individual judge's preference. The customary issue grandparents participate in is the custody/visitation aspect of the case. Beware of provisions for attorney fees. Refer to Fee chapter. The statute specifically states grandparents. The statute does not mention step-grandparents, but some judges do not make this distinction. A step-grandparent may be as bonded to the child as the biological grandparent. The quality of the bonding and the relationship between the party and the child is the most important issue.

If the grandparent becomes aware that the non-custodial parent is paying child support through the local District Attorney Family Support Division, it must be assumed that paternity has been established. You should be able to obtain the case number by calling the District Attorney's office. The case number should be mentioned in your pleadings to the court to show that paternity has already been established if the grandparent intends to file for visitation.

Where to File the Motion for Joinder - Jurisdiction

The court of jurisdiction over grandparent custody and visitation in a joinder situation is where the original underlying custody action was filed. The grandparent "joins" this action for purposes of establishing their own visitation rights.

LEGAL TEST

Legal Test for Independent Petitions and Joinder

The basic legal test for visitation by a grandparent is what is in the **best interest** of the child. This legal test is used by the mediators and the judges to determine what custody and visitation plan is suited best for the child. This test is based on the statutory language.

Maintaining consistency and continuity are considered to be in a child's best interest. This is why the grandparents' visitation law was introduced by Gary Condit while in the California State Assembly. Sometimes parents going through a divorce try to exclude the other spouse's parents from having contact with the grandchild. The law insures that this does not happen.

Since the legal test is what is in the best interest of the child, the goal of mediation is to try to determine if the grandparents have been actively involved in the child's life. The mediator will attempt to evaluate the level of hostility between the grandparent and the custodial parent. They will try to help the parents and grandparents shape a visitation plan which provides for consistency and continuity of contact with the grandparent for the child.

The mediator will attempt to determine the quality of contact between the grandchild and the grandparent. This may include questions about whether or not a grandparent frequently attended the child's extra-curricular activities. If so, this should continue. If a grandparent has provided child care on a regular basis, this should continue. (This presumes, of course, that the custodial parent and the grandparent have an amicable relationship). If the child has always spent extended time with the grandparent during the time when the child is out of school, both parents will be encouraged to continue this relationship.

There are times when a grandparent may not be considered an acceptable candidate for visitation. In the following examples, the grandparents **would not** be considered eligible for visitation. One example is when both parents object to the visitation. Another example is when the parent who has sole legal and sole physical custody objects to the grandparent having visitation. The third example is where there is no order for custody, but the custodial parent objects to visitation by a grandparent. This does not mean the grandparent cannot have a trial in front of a judge. During the trial, the grandparent will present evidence to show **it is** in the grandchild's best interests to have contact with the grandparent.

MEDIATION

Mediation Purpose and Process

In 1984 legislation was passed to require each county to develop a mediation program to assist the parents of children in developing a custody arrangement. This same rule also applied to grandparent visitation. Mediation is mandatory and all parties must participate in the process. Each county was given the option of selecting which model of mediation they wanted to implement. Mediation models have common components. At the end of this book is the California County Chart which was created after contacting county officials. Be sure to review the chart to understand the mediation process in your county. Some counties require mediation before the first court appearance, some at the first court appearance, and some after the first court appearance.

Who Participates in Mediation

Mediation will be conducted in each visitation case where there is a disagreement between the parties. The session includes the parties and the mediator. Step-parent and/or the child are usually not included unless specified by the mediator.

Attorneys Allowed or Not Allowed

Some counties allow attorneys to participate in mediation. Other counties prohibit attorneys from being present. Mediation occurs in the courthouse or in the private offices of the mediators. Mediators may be county employees or independent contractors. Large counties have a large staff of mediators

Small counties have only one mediator on contract to see the parties, usually in the mediator's office. Some mediators have private practices and some are full-time county employees. In some counties, mediators are called evaluators.

Confidential or Non-Confidential Mediation

Mediation can be confidential or non-confidential. In counties where the confidential model has been selected, the mediator is prohibited from sharing any information revealed in the mediation process. In the non-confidential model, the mediator can reveal the information to the judge and can testify about what was said in mediation.

Recommendation or Non-Recommendation Models

Counties have selected either recommendation or non-recommendation models for mediation. In a recommendation county, the mediator will tell the judge what visitation plan would serve the best interest of the child. In a non-recommendation county, the mediator will work with the parties to reach an agreement. If no agreement is reached, the parties proceed to a hearing in front of the judge.

Separate Mediation

If there is an allegation of a history of domestic violence, any party (including a grandparent) can ask to meet with the mediator out of the presence of the other parties. If you desire separate mediation, mention it to the mediator immediately before going into mediation. Sometimes the mediator may want to meet with all parties together before determining if the case requires separate mediation. Separate mediation then proceeds by way of "caucusing" with the mediator either going to each of the parties or having the parties come into the mediation room individually.

Orientation

The purpose of the orientation is to outline the content of the discussions in mediation and help the parties focus on the best interests of the child. Some counties have orientation for the parties and the children. Other counties have orientation for the parties only. Some smaller counties have no formal orientation program. Each county has handouts of printed material to help parties participate effectively in mediation. Some counties require the parties to attend orientation before they can participate in mediation. Orientation can be at the courthouse or some other location.

First Appearance in Mediation

The first actual visit to a mediator is for an assessment. Counties may call the session by specific names, but the underlying purpose is to determine if the parties can reach an agreement. If the parties reach an agreement, the mediation process is over.

The Visitation Plan

Developing the Visitation Plan. It is important for you to understand the custody and visitation plan that is in effect between the parents of the child. By understanding this, you have an excellent opportunity to carve out your "special niche" in the life of your grandchild. The following ideas are new and innovative and (I believe) inspiring. Mediators have struggled with designing plans for grandparents that are not too intrusive on the custodial or non-custodial parents' time. This can cause conflict and ongoing hostilities. On the other hand, they have also attempted to maintain some constant level of contact with the grandparent.

Remember to keep the age of the grandchild in mind. The accepted rule is, the younger the child, the more frequent, less lengthy, the visit should be. For example, you may be rejected if you want to take an infant for a long period of time.

The natural breaks for INCREASED time are:
- infancy to two years old;
- two years old through preschool (five);
- five to ten or eleven; and
- adolescence.

Appropriate orders for infants and preschoolers will certainly be different from orders for adolescents.

If there is more than one grandchild, consider special plans for each grandchild alone if there are large age differences between the grandchildren. If the grandchildren stay with a sitter after school and you are available, you may want to have one of the grandchildren for one day and the other grandchild on another day. Emphasize in mediation that you are sincere about maintaining your bond with the grandchild. Be sure to deal with any issues about your being closely "allied" with your own child. Grandparent visitation is your time with the grandchild.

Weekend and Midweek Plan of the Parents

Most visitation plans contain weekend visitations with some midweek contact if both parents are local. If the parents are geographically separated, the midweek contact may not be possible. If it is possible for you to exercise a midweek visitation that normally would have been your child's, ask for a regular schedule such as each Wednesday (maybe overnight). Be prepared to take the grandchild to school the next day. Also, be prepared to help with any homework.

Parents frequently alternate weekends because it is usually non-work time. The time can vary - - standard is Friday from 6:00 p.m. to Sunday at 6:00 p.m. Weekends can also be defined as the non-custodial parent's day off, i.e., Thursday through Saturday or Saturday through Monday. They may also be defined on a more limited basis: weekends defined as Saturday morning until Sunday evening. Orders may have the weekends defined as first and third to one parent, with second and fourth to the other parent. The fifth weekends are usually shared or alternated.

Your Plan For Weekend Contact

Remember, there are four fifth weekends in a year. Look at the calendar and you will see that there will be five Fridays in four different months of the year. These are spread throughout the year. They are not usually in consecutive months. If your child's visitation plan calls for visitation every other weekend, a logical request would be that one parent have the first and third weekends, and that the other parent has the second and fourth weekends. This leaves four weekends per year for you - the fifth weekend. In effect, each parent would be allowing you to have four of their days each year - not a large request of either parent.

If there is a concern about one of the parents giving up an entire weekend, offer to share one of the days. For example, if one of the parents takes the grandchild to church, offer to make the grandchild available for church services during your weekend.

Which weekends? Be specific. Weekends should be defined as the first weekend having the first Friday of the month in it. Subsequently, the fifth weekend is any month that has five Fridays. The weekend starting with the fifth Friday would be yours. Even if Saturday is the first day of the next month, the preceding definition would keep the dates clear.

When does the weekend begin and end? ·Always be prepared to have some explanation for your selection. Experience has shown that it is better to take the grandchild at meal times. This works as a great icebreaker. This allows you to go get something to eat or take the grandchild to your home to eat.

Midweek Visitation

This may be a nice option for a grandparent. As mentioned earlier, if your own child is unable to exercise midweek visitation (because of the distance or scheduling problems) then you might request a regular day per week. Even if your own child has a regular midweek visitation, there is no reason why you cannot carve a "midweek niche" of your own. Here is a list of suggestions:

- ✓ Volunteer to take care of the grandchild for the primary custodial parent if you are available.
- ✓ Suggest that you pick them up from school and the custodial parent can pick them up at your house.
- ✓ Consider asking if you can take them from their usual babysitter during the time that the custodial parent is working for your "special time" with the grandchild.
- ✓ Volunteer to take the grandchild back to daycare for pick up by the custodial parent at their usual time.
- ✓ Ask if you can watch the grandchild while the parent goes to evening classes or activities.
- ✓ Consider doing the child care in their home. (DON'T SNOOP!!!)
- ✓ Your midweek might be during the afternoon when the grandchild is out of school anyway. If there is an objection to this, change your strategy.
- ✓ Ask for the SIP or In-service days. These are days the grandchild would not normally be in child care anyway.

✓   Some schools have intermittent minimum days due to weather or other events. Ask to be notified in advance of minimum days (by the school) and ask that this time be designated as your time.

✓   Volunteer to take the grandchild to their doctors' and dentists' appointments if you are available.

✓   Ask if you can be notified to pick up the grandchild from school if they are ill. This situation is always an instant and immediate crisis for working parents.

✓   If the grandchild needs to be delivered to a birthday party or school activity, ask if you can provide the transportation. If there is no objection, ask the parents to list you on school documents as a person who can be contacted to chauffeur the grandchild to activities.

✓   Volunteer to be an assistant to the custodial parent as the homeroom mother in the grandchild's classes. You could provide the items that are needed and fill in until the custodial parent arrives.

Holidays and other Special Occasions

Three day weekends. Three day holiday weekends are usually shared between the parties. Generally, the Friday or Monday directly preceding or following a weekend goes to the parent having the weekend. There are days that the grandchild is out of school on three day weekends, however, when the parents have to work. Ask if those days can be assigned to you.

Ask for the traditional holidays that we now celebrate as a Monday holiday. For example, **Memorial Day** is the 30th day of May, which falls on a Monday once every seven years. **Washington's Birthday** is not celebrated as a Monday holiday, but is considered by some businesses to be a non-work day. If neither parent has asked for it, request that you get **Washington's Birthday** since they are getting **President's Day** and **Lincoln's Birthday**.

Before you go to mediation, it is a good idea to go to the grandchild's school to get the school schedule so that you can identify the opportunities for visitation on school holidays following a weekend. Be prepared to discuss your plans for that day so there is an indication you have planned that day to be very special.

Some student-in-service training days may not be on the annual school calendar since it may not be planned in advance. Ask the school secretary to give you any information about other non-school days if you do not see them on the school calendar.

The grandchild's birthday is seldom set apart from the established visitation schedule. Each parent is encouraged to have a birthday party on the weekend of visitation either directly before or after the actual birthday. This may be an opportunity for you to have special time with the grandchild. For example, if the grandchild goes to daycare after school, ask if you can pick up the grandchild on the grandchild's birthday until the custodial parent gets off work or is available to get the grandchild. Have your own special birthday party.

- Ask to have the grandchild on your birthday for a few hours for dinner.
- Volunteer to make sure homework gets done if it is on a weekday since this is always one of the concerns of the custodial parent.
- Ask if you can telefax messages or E-mail the grandchild if the custodial parent has a computer.
- Mention that you would like to send special cards to the grandchild and make sure that the custodial parent agrees to give the card to the grandchild.
- Ask for the Saturday afternoon that a new Disney movie comes out.

During the negotiation to come up with some quality time for the grandparent, mediators frequently appear to feel limited to the traditional type of visitation models. There is a wealth of times available to be with your grandchild without the unwelcome intrusion the custodial parent may feel when too many weekends or vacation times are invaded. Some of these days and times you might consider are as follows:

Valentine's Day. This day can occur any day of the week. It is always February 14th. Consider asking for the grandchild for part of the day. Since this will only occur on a weekday five out of seven years, there should be no strong objection. Talk about looking forward to baking a "heart" cake or cupcakes with a young grandchild.

Saint Patrick's Day. This day always occurs on March 17th and is a "green" day that can be special to you and your grandchild.

Good Friday. Parents seldom have Good Friday off work, but the traditional and year-round schools have the Friday preceding Easter Sunday as a non-school day every year.

Grandparent Day. How can they refuse? Offer to share it with the other side's parent if they are available.

The list goes on and on. Be creative. How about asking to take the grandchild fishing on the vernal equinox and camping on the summer solstice? On Earth Day, you could plan on taking them to a local park for special events when they get out of school. (Always remember to volunteer to get their homework done.)

May Day with the children could mean finding a local event that includes a Maypole. This also occurs on weekdays and weekends.

Halloween is seldom requested by the non-custodial parent. This could be an additional special time for you. Halloween is always October 31st. The parents who decide to share Halloween usually split it into early and late sections. For example, the early section might be from 5:00 p.m. until 6:30 p.m. and the late section might be from 6:30 p.m. until 8:00 p.m. If your own child has not requested to share Halloween, ask for that time to be designated as your time with the grandchild.

The sharing should also be dependent on the age of the grandchild. A school age grandchild should always have enough time to do homework. An infant may have a very early bedtime. Have the cousins or other family members participate in your visitation, if that is something that you usually would have done.

Your visitation could include special activities that are unique to you as a grandparent. For example, you might consider teaching the boy or girl how to fish, hunt, use tools, make things, go on field trips in your own backyard or a park. You might let the grandchild have a favorite animal at your home. This could be very special to the grandchild, especially if they live in an apartment and do not have the capacity for pets where they live.

Christmas Day and **Christmas Eve** are generally rotated between the parents. It is assumed that your child will share the grandchild with you during this very special day.

However, another opportunity for personal time is when the grandchild is out of school for the two weeks around Christmas. Ask if you can have the grandchild during the day and maybe an overnight or two during this period of time. If there are an uneven number of days from the day that school lets out until the day before school resumes, ask for the odd day. If each parent is to have the children for seven days and there are eighteen non-school days, ask for the extra ones. This is another reason it is important to be conversant with the child's school schedule.

Remember, consistency in the grandchild's life is foremost for their development. Consistency and continuity, without hostility, are ideal. If there is conflict during the exchange of the grandchild, the grandchild gets upset and may develop loyalty conflicts. If this occurs on a regular basis, the grandchild deteriorates and may be referred to a therapist.

If the therapist determines that the grandchild is traumatized by the exchange of the grandchild at the grandparent's visitation, a recommendation may be made to limit the contact. The recommendation may also be to terminate visitation by the grandparent.

Enough cannot be said about staying neutral with the parent who is opposing your visitation. It may even be necessary for you to see a therapist in post-dissolution issues in order to fully understand how your role could be undermined by a custodial parent.

Do not carry tales back to your child about your concerns when the grandchild is with you, unless those concerns are so great that there should be some legal intervention. For example, if you mention to your son that "Little Johnny" has a bruise on his leg, your son might confront the mother about committing child abuse.

If your grandchild does show symptoms of abuse or neglect, deal with it like you would if it were not your grandchild and you were just providing child care. For example, if the grandchild has a black eye and belt welts all over his or her body, it is appropriate to call the police and child protective services. It does not matter if it is your grandchild or any other child.

Keeping neutral also allows the grandchild to share information with you that perhaps cannot be shared with warring parents. This confidence should be maintained. A grandchild needs what grandparents provide - love.

No Agreement at First Appearance

If the parties do not reach an agreement, the case is usually recessed for some form of further evaluation. This can be with the mediator or with a child custody evaluator. The child custody evaluator may be a court employee or a local mental health professional who understands the best interests of the child.

In a recommendation county, the mediator may recommend to the judge what visitation plan should be in effect until the mediation process is completed. In a non-recommendation county, the parties will have a short hearing in front of the judge to determine what the interim plan should be. At the hearing, in a confidential county, the mediator cannot testify about any information obtained in mediation. In a non-confidential county, the mediator may testify about what was said in mediation and where the negotiation broke down.

The parties may be ordered to meet with an evaluator or mediator to continue to work on an agreement. If the parties reach an agreement during this further process, then mediation is concluded. The moving party (the person that initiated the action) is required to prepare the order of the court, unless the court has the facility to prepare it. The moving party should request a copy of the minute order (which is a document prepared by the judge's clerk) from the court clerk's office a day or two after the hearing. The formal order is usually prepared on a document called a Findings and Order After Hearing. This can be obtained from the clerk's office. It is prepared and then submitted to the judge for signature. When it is returned from the clerk, copies should be mailed to all parties. If the parties continue to disagree on the custodial arrangement for the child, the judge will set the case for trial. The language the judge uses for the case is "set to the long cause calendar."

Family Court Investigator

Sometimes in the assessment stage, it becomes apparent from the allegations made by the parties that a formal investigation needs to be initiated. This investigation is similar to the one conducted in a guardianship action. The criteria for the investigation include any allegations that affect parenting, i.e., drugs, alcoholism, physical and sexual abuse. There may also be an allegation of illegal activities in the home.

During assessment, the mediator may recess the case for the investigation. This usually takes thirty days and as much as ninety days to complete. The mediator may make a recommendation for visitation pending the investigation pursuant to the above criteria. The family court investigator may interview or review reports from the police department, child protective services, teachers, social workers or anyone else who has had contact with the child. If you have documents in your possession that have a bearing on the case, be sure that these documents are turned into the investigator quickly. If you know of any proceedings in any other county or for any other type of case related to the grandchild or parties, give the investigator that information as well. During the time that the investigation is being conducted, if you become aware of pertinent information, such as a recent arrest of a party, it is important that the investigator gets this information. If there is a fee for the investigation, the judge decides who pays the fee and will make an order either after the judge receives the investigative report or at trial.

At the end of the investigation, the parties return to mediation or evaluation for a review of the investigator's report. If both parties agree with the investigator's recommendation, the judge may make orders accordingly and the case is concluded. If either party disagrees with the investigator's recommendation, the case is added to the long cause calendar in the same manner as mentioned above.

There are instances where the parties are referred back to mediation after the investigator's report has been completed. The mediator may then use the report as a reference to help the parties work through their custody/visitation plan. If the parties are still unable to agree, the mediator may make a recommendation that incorporates the investigator's report or make a different recommendation that will be in effect pending the long cause trial. In a non-recommendation county, the judge will decide on the interim plan.

Appointment of Attorney for Child

In extreme cases of hostility between the parties, the court may appoint an independent attorney to represent the child. The presumption is that the parties are not acting in the child's best interest. Each court should have a list of local family law attorneys who are eligible for appointment. To understand the law regarding appointing the attorney for the child, please refer to the California Family Code, Section 3150 and thereafter.

Supervised Visitation Requested During Mediation

If there is an allegation of sexual or physical abuse of the grandchild, any party may ask that the alleged offending party's time with the grandchild be supervised by a neutral third party. If you are going to request supervised visitations, be prepared to name a number of people who would be willing to supervise. Also, speak with your potential supervisors before coming to court and find out what their availability is as far as how much time they could commit to the supervision. There is a new law effective January 1, 1998, which sets forth the rules for a supervised visitation. A copy of the new law and the appropriate Penal Code is found at the end of this book. The supervisors must be familiar with the rules before supervision occurs.

Grandparents may be asked to supervise visitation. However, it is highly unlikely that other relatives will be allowed to supervise unless the alleged offending party agrees.

Know Your Buzzwords

The mediators are trained as child psychologists, marriage counselors or have other certifications dealing with the psychological aspects of relationships. They use common "buzzwords" that have special meaning to them. For a grandparent to communicate effectively, it is important to know the words and the meanings they import.

The law itself has "buzzwords." However, these are called "legal terms of art." A copy of the law which defines the variations of types of custody is at the end of this book. You should read it to become familiar with the terms.

Below are two terms that might be used in mediation and how they are generally defined. Custody orders or language may not be appropriate in a grandparent visitation case. It is assumed that the custody of the grandchild is with the parents. Visitation with the grandchild will be with the non-custodial parent and the grandparent. Understanding the terms, however, may give you guidance and insight in how to work with the parents to help them implement the plan.

Temperamental Fit -- this is not a temper tantrum. This phrase is used to describe the temperament of the grandchild being more closely related to one parent or the other. This phrase came from a research document which indicates that the better the temperamental fit with the parent, the better the grandchild adjusts to a custody/visitation plan.

Primary Parent -- this term is used to identify the parent who has been the primary provider of the day-to-day needs of the grandchild. Mediators frequently ask questions of the parents to reach some understanding about which parent has been the primary parent.

Words of Wisdom

I have asked mediators for a simple statement to guide parents and grandparents entering the mediation process.

> "Divorce never terminates relationships where children are involved. It only changes the relationship between family members."

> "Try to keep in mind that unless there is abuse involved, a shared relationship with both parents and grandparents is in the child's best interest."

> "Communicate; communicate, communicate, communicate."

> "Cooperate on any issues regarding your children and grandchildren."

Each mediator has a particular style in obtaining information. Some mediators use a "bottom line" approach. They are not interested in hearing the details of any problems. They only want to discuss the proposal for settlement.

Some will let the parties talk for some time before asking questions. Others will ask questions and focus on the answers. Try to be sensitive to your particular mediator's information gathering style. One of the easiest ways to "blow" your case is to be too focused on you and what you want to say. Remember, mediators do this weekly and have developed their skills at reading different situations and the parties.

Family Code Terms

Studies have shown that very small children can become disoriented if there is too much repetitive change in the environment. Studies also show that joint custody works best when the parents get along well together and the transition between the parents' homes is comfortable for the child. The same rules apply to grandparent visitation.

Legal Custody - This can be joint or sole. This term addresses the legal rights of the parents. Except in rare cases, joint legal custody is preferred. One example in the importance of joint legal custody is if the "visiting" parent has the child when the child has a non-life-threatening incident (such as a major cut that requires stitches). In the case of joint legal custody, the parent with the child can authorize the attending physician to treat the child immediately. In the case of sole legal custody, the doctor or hospital could require the parent assigned sole legal custody to sign the authorization forms before treating the child. Grandparents usually do not participate in legal custody. A grandparent should have a "Caregiver Authorization" signed by both parents when the grandchild is in their care and control. A model of this document is found in the attachment section at the end of this book.

Joint legal custody also assures (but does not require) access to medical, dental, and other health care related records. This includes school records as well. There is a federal law and a state law which addresses the rights of both parents to access school records. A copy of the federal law is attached. The state law is included in the California Family Code which is an attachment at the end of this book.

Physical Custody - This is where the child lives. The person with physical custody generally has the child the majority of the time. The other parent has various periods of time which are addressed by different descriptions depending on the language used by the mediator. There is a trend in the state to get away from addressing the out-of-custody parent as the parent with "visitation." The language itself creates a feeling of lack of involvement or commitment to the child. One suggestion by the State Bar Family Law Section was that each parent's share of "custody" would be defined as periods of "care and responsibility." Some mediators tend to think along the lines of each parent having a share of custody, while others still talk about custody and visitation. It generally doesn't matter what you call it (unless welfare is involved). What matters is how it works.

Sometimes the parents will dispute what to call the physical custody. Some parents feel better with terms like "joint physical custody" with one parent designated as the primary caretaker. Or, "shared physical custody" with one parent designated as the primary caretaker. Some agreements are reached where the custody is called either joint or shared with neither parent designated as primary caretaker. The primary caretaker designation is absolutely essential in cases where there is a recipient of Aid to Families with Dependent Children (welfare). Otherwise, it is not necessary to designate a primary caretaker. There can be abuse of the designation "primary caretaker." Some parents have used this designation to exclude the other parent's input. Remember, this designation is only necessary in welfare cases. It does not give the parent any extra decision making ability.

One thing to keep in mind is that mediators believe that parents, along with the people who love the child, will make the best decisions for their child if they understand the child's needs. The way this frequently works out is the mediators will recommend that the parents continue to do what they were doing prior to coming into mediation. The grandparent's time with the child may be referred to as visitation or periods of care, custody and control.

If you have been involved in your grandchild's life during the time the marriage was intact, give some careful thought to what this involvement looked like in terms of days and hours. It may not be possible to duplicate it because of the parents vying for time. It is even better for you if you managed to maintain the relationship with both of the parents and stayed involved up until the mediation.

Restraining Orders

Some clients feel the need to get restraining orders as "part and parcel" of working through a plan for sharing. It is common for restraining orders to be agreed upon during the mediation process.

This is the list of restraining orders the mediator may have in his or her possession during the mediation process. If there are additional restraining orders that you feel are needed, write them out and mention them to the mediator. Where you see mother and father listed, grandmother and grandfather may be inserted.

- No party shall discuss court proceedings in the presence of the child except to inform them of the court's order.

- No party shall annoy, molest, harass, or disturb the other's peace.

- Each party shall stay at least 100 yards away from the other party's residence/place of employment except for peaceful contacts regarding the minor child.

- No party shall remove the child from the State of California.

- No party shall change the child's current county of residence without forty-five (45) days prior written notice to the other party.

- No party shall use illegal substances during his or her period of care and control of the minor child or for twenty-four (24) hours prior thereto, nor permit the child to be in presence of illegal substances.

- The Mother/Father shall undergo urine drug screening at the designated laboratory on   /   /   before 5:00 p.m. at the expense of the Mother/Father. Results shall be sent to the Mediator/Attorneys/Mother/Father.

- The Mother/Father shall undergo random drug screening at a designated lab during regular business hours within 8/12/24 hours of a request which will be made by Mother/Father through the Attorneys/Mediator/Parties, at the expense of the Mother/Father. Results shall be sent to the Mediator/Attorneys/Mother/Father.

- No party will consume alcohol to excess during his or her period of care and control of the minor child or for 8/12/24 hours prior thereto.

- If the restriction concerning drug use or alcohol use is violated as determined by law enforcement or laboratory test, that period of the violating party's care and control of the minor child shall be forfeited.

- Any party may be the child-care provider of first choice if the custodial parent is absent for more than an overnight. The minor child shall be returned to the custodial parent at the conclusion of this period of absence.

- Each party shall keep the other informed of the names, addresses, and telephone numbers of all child-care providers.

- Each party shall keep the other parties informed of all appointments for the minor child with all health-care providers.

- The party ending their period of care and control of the child shall arrange transportation.

- The Father/Mother/Grandparent shall arrange transportation at the beginning/ending of their period of care and control of the child for midweek/weekends/non-school attendance periods/holidays.

- Unless otherwise mutually agreed, the places of exchange shall be the residences of each party.

- Each party shall remain in their respective vehicles at the time of exchange.

- If Mother/Father/Grandparent is in excess of ___minutes late to exchange without prior notice, that person's care and control of the minor child is forfeited.

- Each party shall notify the other immediately of any emergency involving the child.

- Each party shall provide a smoke free environment for the child and not allow the child to be in a closed environment where anyone is smoking.

TRIAL
Visitation Trial
When the parties do not reach an agreement at any phase of mediation, the next step is a visitation trial. The case is added to the "long cause calendar" which means that the case will go to trial. Sometimes, parties settle on the courthouse steps. It is <u>never</u> too late to reach an agreement. If an agreement is reached, the agreement is recited to the judge and the agreement becomes the order of the court.

On the trial date, the cases are called in the order they appear on the calendar. Child custody cases are usually given priority over other types of civil cases and are called first after criminal jury and criminal court trials. If there is a courtroom available, the parties and their attorneys proceed to the department where the case has been assigned. If there is no courtroom available immediately, the parties are put on "trailing" status and must be available to be ready to proceed to trial on short notice.

If you are placed on trailing status and if you do not have an attorney, you are directed to tell the master calendar clerk where you can be reached. After you are called, you are expected to be in the courtroom where the case has been assigned on short notice.

Each attorney has different methods of dealing with the "trailing calendar": some stay with their clients, some have their clients wait in their office, some take care of other cases and have their clients remain at a designated location.

When the trial judge calls the case, the party who does not agree with the temporary order made by the judge or with the mediator's/family court investigator's recommendation has the obligation to start the trial. They usually testify first about why they disagree. In a non-recommendation county, the person requesting visitation would start first.

Frequently, child custody trials become a "battle of experts". The person disagreeing with the judge's order in a non-recommendation county or the mediator's recommendation may have their own mental health therapist testify about why the recommendation is wrong.

The party who agrees with the judge's temporary orders or mediator's recommendation usually subpoenas the mediator to testify on their behalf. Additional witnesses may include friends, relatives, or other professionals who have firsthand knowledge of their interaction with the child.

At the conclusion of the trial, the court may rule from the bench or take the matter under submission. Taking a case under submission means that the judge will mail the order to the attorneys or the party, if there is no attorney. The judge is allowed up to ninety days to give the ruling.

Chapter Three

GUARDIANSHIP CASES

The underlying philosophy in guardianship cases is to provide a safe environment for children when the child's parents are unable or unwilling to do so.

TYPE ONE - PROBATE COURT

BASIS FOR REQUESTING A GUARDIANSHIP

A guardianship may not be necessary. If the only problem is enrolling the child in school or providing medical care, then the only requirement is the document called the Caregiver's Authorization. A Caregiver's Authorization is included in the list of attachments in the back of this book. Guardianships are different in many ways from grandparent visitation rights even though it may be a grandparent requesting to be appointed as a guardian. The usual guardianship case is where both parents are unfit or unavailable to care for the child. For example, if both parents are drug addicts and unable to care for the child, a guardianship is the appropriate lawsuit. If the parents are incarcerated, then a grandparent usually petitions for a guardianship.

If both parents are in an accident and cannot care for the grandchild, a guardianship is the method by which another person can obtain custody. During Desert Storm, guardianships were granted because the parents were in active military duty. Guardianships can be granted whether or not the parents are married or whether or not they are living together or have ever lived together.

LEGAL TEST

The legal test for grandparent guardianship is different from the legal test for visitation. The legal test for grandparent visitation is what visitation is in the grandchild's best interest. The **legal test** for guardianship is whether leaving the grandchild with either parent is **detrimental to the child**. Detriment can have different meanings depending on the circumstances. There is <u>no specific legal definition</u> in the statutes. There are different levels of detriment which allows a guardianship to be granted.

No Obvious Detriment

An example of this would be when the parent of the grandchild lives with the parents and they are willing to support him or her. The grandchild's parent may want to go to school and is willing to allow the grandparents to have the guardianship. Another example is when the grandparents want to put the grandchild on health insurance. This usually is not possible unless there is a guardianship in place.

Presumed Detriment

These are situations where no direct abuse of the child needs to be proved. These situations would be drug abuse, sexual abuse of other children, spousal abuse, and other patterns of behavior which in and of itself renders the parent incapable of being a fit parent. The act itself is of such detriment that no connection to the child need be established.

Environment Detriment

In this type of detriment, there may be no specific finding against the parent. The detriment may stem from an unstable home environment. The long term lodging of a child with a non-parent to whom the child grows attached may be the basis for a request for guardianship by the non-parent. The child may also be with a parent, but be surrounded with other undesirable persons with criminal and/or drug histories. A non-parent may be abusive to the child and the parent cannot or will not protect the child from the abuse.

Direct Detriment

This is direct involvement by the natural parent in preventing the child from being brought up in a normal, stable, safe environment. This would include physical, sexual, and mental abuse of the child. It would also include neglect of the child's food, clothing, shelter and hygiene, as well as seeing to the proper education and medical treatment of the child.

An isolated incident does not determine detriment. There are other considerations such as the remoteness of the particular act. A drug conviction twenty years ago would not mean much, but one within the last year would be very significant. A prior conviction of child molestation without subsequent treatment might, in itself, be sufficient for finding detriment.

The very personable local court investigator in Stanislaus County (where I practice) thinks the legislature was wise in not statutorily defining detriment. There are situations where detriment must be defined as Justice Potter Stewart described pornography, "I can't define it, but I know it when I see it."

PROCESS

A petition for guardianship is filed with the probate court, not the family law court. At the time of filing, a hearing date is assigned, usually forty-five days away. Copies of the pleadings, along with a personal history questionnaire, are provided to the county office doing the guardianship investigation.

If there is an emergency situation, a petition for the appointment of a temporary guardian shall be filed and presented to the court for signature. The parents must be notified of the application for the temporary guardianship and the application for the general guardianship. If the parents object to the temporary guardianship, they can call the investigator and request an immediate hearing.

The personal history questionnaire is used to conduct background checks on the petitioners, the parents, and any other adult(s) living in the proposed guardian's home. The purpose of the investigation, as it relates to the proposed guardian(s), is to actually see what is going on with the child and to see the child in the environment where the child will be living. The purpose of investigating the parents is to substantiate the accusations and prove or disprove that leaving the child with the parent(s) would be detrimental.

At the conclusion of the investigation, the investigator writes a recommendation to the probate judge either recommending the guardianship be granted or denied. The recommendation could also be that the guardianship is granted until one of the borderline parents develops better parenting skills. The report will tell the results and the extent of the investigation which caused the final recommendation to be made.

If the guardianship investigator recommends that the grandparent be named guardian, the probate judge may make orders at the guardianship hearing. If either parent objects to the granting of the guardianship, then the parties (a proposed guardian and biological parent) may be referred to the family law court to participate in mediation.

In guardianship proceedings, the mediation process is identical in concept with the mediation visitation proceedings. In the case of guardianship, however, the visitation plan will be addressed to the parent objecting to the guardianship. The mediator's role is to provide definition to the recommendations of the investigation.

MEDIATION

Mediation Purpose and Process

In 1984, legislation was passed to require each county to develop a mediation program to assist the parents of children in developing a custody arrangement. This same rule also covers guardianship cases. Mediation is mandatory and all parties must participate in the process. Each county was given the option of selecting which model of mediation they wanted to implement. Mediation models have common components. At the end of this book is the California County Chart which was created by contacting each county's officials. Be sure to review the chart to understand the mediation process in your county.

Who Participates in Mediation

Mediation will be conducted in each guardianship case where there is a disagreement between the parties about the guardianship investigator's recommendation. The mediation session includes the parties and the mediator. Stepparents and the grandchild are usually not included unless requested by the mediator.

Attorneys Allowed or Not Allowed

Some counties allow attorneys to participate in mediation. Other counties prohibit attorneys from being present. Mediation occurs in the courthouse or in the private offices of the mediators. Mediators may be county employees or independent contractors. Large counties have a large number of mediators on staff. Small counties have only one mediator on contract to see the parties, usually in their private office. Some mediators have private practices and some are full-time county employees.

Confidential or Non-Confidential Mediation

Mediation can be confidential or non-confidential. In counties where the confidential model has been selected, the mediator is prohibited from sharing any information revealed in the mediation process. In the non-confidential model, the mediator can reveal the information to the judge, and may testify about what was said in mediation.

Recommendation or Non-Recommendation Models

Counties have selected either recommendation or non-recommendation models for mediation. In a recommending county, the mediator will tell the court what visitation plan would serve the best interests of the child. In a non-recommending county, the mediator will work with the parties to reach an agreement. If no agreement is reached, the parties proceed to a hearing in front of the judge. In guardianship cases, the mediator may or may not inform the court about the outcome of mediation. Some counties only use the guardianship investigator's report to determine what visitation schedule the parents should have.

Separate Mediation

If there is an allegation of a history of domestic violence, any party (including a grandparent) can ask to meet with the mediator out of the presence of the other parties. If you desire separate mediation, mention it to the mediator immediately before going into mediation. Sometimes the mediator may want to meet with all parties together before determining that the case requires separate mediation. The mediation then proceeds by way of "caucusing" with the mediator either going to each of the parties or having the parties come into the mediation room individually.

Orientation

In guardianship cases, the judge may require the parties to go to orientation prior to proceeding with mediation. Some counties have orientation for the parties and the children. Other counties have orientation for the parties only. Each county has handouts of printed material to help parties participate effectively in mediation.

Some counties require the parties attend orientation before they can participate in mediation. Orientation can be at the courthouse or some other location. The purpose of the orientation is to outline the content of the discussions in mediation and help the parties focus on the best interest of the child.

First Appearance in Mediation

The first actual visit to a mediator is for a form of assessment. Counties may call the session by specific names, but the underlying purpose is to determine if the parties can reach an agreement. If the parties reach an agreement, the mediation process is over. The order appointing guardian is prepared and letters of guardianship are issued by the probate judge.

Sometimes the mediation order is a graduating-type order, such as starting with one visit of a few hours to increase over time. The recommendation by the investigator may include some significant steps that the parents have to make before having a "normal" visitation schedule. Sometimes the granting or escalating of visitation is contingent upon the parents' participation in a parenting and/or drug rehabilitation program. Other orders may include that visitation may only occur in the presence of the guardian until the parents obtain suitable housing. Sometimes restraining orders regarding the use of alcohol will be made if one of the parents has a drinking problem. The same is true with regard to drugs.

Understanding the range of possible visitation orders may be useful, but guardianships are usually granted on a direct or implied finding of unfitness. "Normal" visitation would not be appropriate for an "unfit" parent. Safeguards for the child must be put in place.

In cases where there should be a supervised visitation between the child and a parent, the guardian may be selected to be the supervisor. If this is impossible for some reason, be prepared to give names of people who could supervise the visitation. You should contact these people before the hearing and make sure you know their availability. You should also inform any potential supervisors that they will be required to go to the mediation orientation (if provided) to fully understand their responsibility as a supervisor. Guardianships can be terminated upon the parent filing a petition to terminate the guardianship. The case may go back to investigation and/or mediation. If there is still a dispute over whether the parents are able or available to provide adequate parenting, the case will go to trial.

If there was **no finding of unfitness** on behalf of the parent, the parent does not have to prove that they are now fit to parent. The legal test would be what is in the **child's best interest**.

If a **finding of unfitness** has been found in the guardianship action, the parent seeking to terminate the guardianship must be able to prove to the court that he or she **is now fit** to assume the responsibilities of caring for the child. This evidence may include proving the parent is now living in a stable environment and has completed the recommended programs for alcohol abuse, drug abuse, or parenting classes. Upon a finding by the court that the parent is no longer unfit, the court will terminate the guardianship. After the trial, if the court finds that either parent is now available and able to parent, then the need for the guardianship is terminated.

Once the guardianship is terminated, a grandparent may want to continue to have specified contact with the child. The feelings between the custodial parent and grandparent may have been bitter over the grandparent's petitioning for guardianship. If the parent who has had the guardianship terminated refuses to agree to a visitation order, the grandparent can still petition for visitation through one of the methods listed in the previous chapter. The order is made in the underlying action involving the parents.

TRIAL
Guardianship Trial

The last stage of the guardianship process occurs when there is a disagreement on the appointment of the guardian. This case is added to the "long cause calendar" which means that the case will go to trial. Sometimes, parties settle on the courthouse steps. It is <u>never</u> too late to reach an agreement. If an agreement is reached, the agreement is recited to a judge and the agreement becomes the order of the court.

On the day of trial, the cases are called in the order they appear on the calendar. Child custody/guardianship cases are usually given priority over other types of civil cases and are called first after criminal jury and criminal court trials. If there is a courtroom available, the parties and their attorneys proceed to the department where the case has been assigned. If there is no courtroom immediately available, the parties are put on "trailing" status and must be available to proceed to trial on short notice.

If you are placed on trailing status and you do not have an attorney, you will be directed to inform the master calendar clerk where you can be reached. After you are called, you are expected to be in the courtroom where the case has been assigned on short notice (fifteen minutes).

Each attorney has different methods of dealing with the "trailing calendar": some stay with their clients, some have their clients wait in their office, some take care of other cases and have their clients remain at a designated location.

When the trial judge calls the case, the party who does not agree with guardianship investigator's recommendation has the obligation to start the trial. They usually testify first about why they disagree with the guardianship investigator's report.

Frequently, child custody trials become a "battle of experts." The person disagreeing with the guardianship investigator's recommendation may have their own mental health therapist testify about why the guardianship investigator's recommendation is wrong.

The party who agrees with the guardianship investigator's recommendation usually subpoenas the investigator to testify on their behalf. Additional witnesses may include friends, relatives, or other professionals who have firsthand knowledge of your interaction with the child.

At the conclusion of the trial, the court may rule from the bench or take the matter under submission. Taking a case under submission means the judge will mail the order to the attorneys or the party, if there is no attorney. The judge is allowed up to ninety days to give the ruling.

TYPE TWO - JUVENILE COURT

The philosophy of guardianships in juvenile court is to provide a safe home for the child who has been a dependent of the court and who does not have parents who are willing and able to provide for the child's care.

BASIS FOR REQUESTING A GUARDIANSHIP

Under certain circumstances, the juvenile court may appoint a guardian. This usually occurs when the parents are not interested in utilizing the services of the juvenile court for reunification with the child. The guardianship is put in place as an alternative to maintaining the child as a dependent of the court. A copy of Welfare and Institutions Code Section 360 can be found at the end of this book.

LEGAL TEST

The legal test for the appointment of a guardian is a determination by the court that a guardianship is in the best interests of the child. The parent must advise the court that the parent is not interested in the services provided by the juvenile court. The parent and the child must agree to the guardianship.

PROCESS

The guardianship order is made at the final hearing when a child has been determined to be a dependent of the court. Rather than the juvenile courts continuing the dependency, the juvenile court appoints a legal guardian and issues letters of guardianship. In order for a grandparent to be appointed as the legal guardian, there must be an assessment prepared by the probation department. The assessment will include the following:

1. Current search efforts for, and notification of, a noncustodial parent in the manner provided in Section 337.

2. A review of the amount of and nature of any contact between the minor and his or her parents since the filing of the petition.

3. An evaluation of the minor's medical, developmental, scholastic, mental, and emotional status.

4. A preliminary assessment of the eligibility and commitment of any identified prospective guardian, particularly the caretaker, to include a social history including a screening for criminal records and prior referrals for child abuse or neglect, the capability to meet the minor's needs, and the understanding of the legal and financial rights and responsibilities of guardianship.

5. The relationship of the minor to any identified prospective guardian, the duration and nature of the relationship, the motivation for seeking guardianship, and a statement from the minor concerning the guardianship, unless the minor's age or physical, emotional, or other condition precludes the minor's meaningful response, and if so, a description of the condition.

6. An analysis of the likelihood that the minor would be adopted if parental rights were terminated.

The person responsible for preparing the assessment may be called and questioned by any party to the guardianship proceeding.

At this guardianship hearing:

(A)   If the court finds that the minor is a person described by Section 300, it may, without adjudicating the minor a dependent child of the court, order that services be provided to keep the family together and place the minor and the minor's parent or guardian under the supervision of the probation officer for a time period consistent with Section 301.

(B)   If the family subsequently is unable or unwilling to cooperate with the services being provided, the probation officer may file a petition with the juvenile court pursuant to Section 332 alleging that a previous petition has been sustained and that disposition pursuant to subdivision (b) has been ineffective in positively changing the situation requiring the child's welfare services. Upon hearing the petition, the court shall order that the petition shall be dismissed or that a new disposition hearing shall be held pursuant to subdivision (d).

(C)   If the court finds that the minor is a person described by Section 300, it may order and adjudge the minor to be a dependent child of the court.

There is no provision in the statute for mediation in guardianship cases in juvenile court proceedings. There are no further court dates after the guardianship is granted. If the parents decide at a later date to file a request to terminate the guardianship, the case would go back to Juvenile Court for a hearing on the request.

Chapter Four

JUVENILE COURT DEPENDENCY PROCEEDINGS

When officials in the county receive information that a child has been injured or is in an unsafe environment, juvenile court proceedings may get underway. The usual way a case will start is a call to Child Protective Services Department (CPS). This may be from a friend or neighbor. It may also be from a police officer that has been called to the residence even for some other reason.

When the worker at CPS receives the call, an on-site visit is made to determine whether or not the child should be removed from the home. Some counties have pilot programs where the CPS workers get the family members together to work out a solution for the at-risk child instead of the case going to juvenile court.

LEGAL TEST

The legal test to determine whether or not the child should be made a dependent child of the court and/or removed from the parents is as follows:

Welfare and Institutions Code Section 300, Minors within Juvenile Court Jurisdiction

Any minor who comes within any of the following descriptions is within the jurisdiction of the juvenile court which may adjudge that person to be a dependent child of the court:

(A)   The minor has suffered, or there is a substantial risk that the minor will suffer, serious physical harm inflicted nonaccidentally upon the minor by the minor's parent or guardian. For the purposes of this subdivision, a court may find there is a substantial risk of serious future injury based on the manner in which a less serious injury was inflicted, a history of repeated inflictions of injuries on the minor or the minor's siblings, or a combination of these and other actions by the parent or guardian which indicate the child is at risk of serious physical harm.

For the purposes of this subdivision, "serious physical harm" does not include reasonable and age-appropriate spanking to the buttocks where there is no evidence of serious physical injury.

(B)   The minor has suffered, or there is a substantial risk that the minor will suffer, serious physical harm or illness, as a result of the failure or inability of his or her parent or guardian to adequately supervise or protect the minor, or the willful or negligent failure of the minor's parent or guardian to adequately supervise or protect the minor from the conduct of the custodian with whom the minor has been left, or by the willful or negligent failure of the parent or guardian to provide the minor with adequate food, clothing, shelter, or medical treatment, or by the inability of the parent or guardian to provide regular care for the minor due to the parent's or guardian's mental illness, developmental disability, or substance abuse. No minor shall be found to be a person described by this subdivision solely due to the lack of an emergency shelter for the family. Whenever it is alleged that a minor comes within the jurisdiction of the court on the basis of the parent's or guardian's willful failure to provide adequate medical treatment or a specific decision to provide spiritual treatment through prayer, the court shall give deference to the parent's or guardian's medical treatment, nontreatment, or spiritual treatment through prayer alone in accordance with the tenets and practices of a recognized church or religious denomination, by an accredited practitioner thereof, and shall not assume jurisdiction unless necessary to protect the minor from suffering serious physical harm or illness.

In making its determination, the court shall consider:
    (1)   the nature of the treatment proposed by the parent or guardian,
    (2)   the risks to the minor posed by the course of treatment or nontreatment proposed by the parent or guardian,
    (3)   the risk, if any, of the course of treatment being proposed by the petitioning agency, and,
    (4)   the likely success of the course of treatment or nontreatment proposed by the parent or guardian and agency. The minor shall continue to be a dependent child pursuant to this subdivision only so long as is necessary to protect the minor from risk of suffering serious physical harm or illness.

(C)   The minor is suffering serious emotional damage, or is at substantial risk of suffering serious emotional damage, evidenced by severe anxiety, depression, withdrawal, or untoward aggressive behavior toward self or others, as a result of the conduct of the parent or guardian or, who has no parent or guardian capable of providing appropriate care. No minor shall be found to be a person described by this subdivision if the willful failure of the parent or guardian to provide adequate mental health treatment is based on a sincerely held religious belief and if a less intrusive judicial intervention is available.

(D)   The minor has been sexually abused, or there is a substantial risk that the minor will be sexually abused, as defined in Section 11165.1 of the Penal Code, by his or her parent or guardian or a member of his or her household, or the parent or guardian has failed to adequately protect the minor from sexual abuse when the parent or guardian knew or reasonably should have known that the minor was in danger of sexual abuse.

(E)   The minor is under the age of five and has suffered severe physical abuse by a parent, or by any person known by the parent, if the parent knew or reasonably should have known that the person was physically abusing the minor. For the purposes of this subdivision, "severe physical abuse" means any of the following: any single act of abuse which causes physical trauma of sufficient severity that, if left untreated, would cause permanent physical disfigurement, permanent physical disability, or death; any single act of sexual abuse which causes significant bleeding, deep bruising, or significant external or internal swelling; or more than one act of physical abuse, each of which causes bleeding, deep bruising, significant external or internal swelling, bone fracture, or unconsciousness; or the willful, prolonged failure to provide adequate food. A minor may not be removed from the physical custody of his or her parent or guardian on the basis of a finding of severe physical abuse unless the probation officer has made an allegation of severe physical abuse pursuant to Section 332.

(F)   The minor's parent or guardian caused the death of another minor through abuse or neglect.

(G)   The minor has been left without any provision for support; the minor's parent has been incarcerated or institutionalized and cannot arrange for the care of the minor; or a relative or other adult custodian with whom the minor resides, or has been left is unwilling or unable to provide care or support for the minor, the whereabouts of the parent is unknown, and reasonable efforts to locate the parent have been unsuccessful.

(H)   The minor has been freed for adoption by one or both parents for 12 months by either relinquishment or termination of parental rights or an adoption petitioner has not been granted.

(I)   The minor has been subjected to an act or acts of cruelty by a parent or guardian or a member of his or her household, or the parent or guardian has failed to adequately protect the minor from an act or acts of cruelty when the parent or guardian knew or reasonably should have known that the minor was in danger of being subjected to an act or acts of cruelty.

(J)   The minor's sibling has been abused or neglected, as defined in subdivision (a), (b), (d), (e), or (I), and there is a substantial risk that the minor will be abused or neglected, as defined in those subdivisions. The court shall consider the circumstances surrounding the abuse or neglect of the sibling, the age and gender of each minor, the nature of the abuse or neglect of the sibling, the mental condition of the parent or guardian, and any other factors the court considers probative in determining whether there is a substantial risk to the minor.

It is the intent of the Legislature that nothing in this section disrupt the family unnecessarily or intrude inappropriately into family life, prohibit the use of reasonable methods of parental discipline, or prescribe a particular method of parenting. Further, nothing in this section is intended to limit the offering of voluntary services to those families in need of assistance but who do not come within the descriptions of this section. To the extent that savings accrues to the state from child welfare services funding obtained as a result of this section, those savings shall be used to promote services which support family maintenance and family reunification plans, such as client transportation, out-of-home respite care, parenting training, and the provision of temporary or emergency in-home caretaker and persons teaching and demonstrating homemaking skills. The Legislature further declares that a physical disability such as blindness or deafness, is no bar to the raising of happy and well-adjusted children and that a court's determination pursuant to this section shall center upon whether a parent's disability prevents him or her from exercising care and control.

As can be seen from the text of the statute, all issues related to the well being and safety of a child come within the statutory definitions. If the child needs to be removed from the home, the statutes also state that the preferred placement is with a relative.

<u>This is usually the first place for involvement by grandparents in juvenile court dependency cases.</u>

If the child is injured or in danger, there is no court hearing to determine whether the child should be removed immediately from the parents. The CPS worker can take immediate custody of the child for placement. The worker will usually ask the parents if there is a relative who would be appropriate to provide care for the minor until the court hearing takes place. If there is a relative capable and willing to take the child, the worker is required by statute to place the child with a relative pending the hearing.

If there is no relative available at that time who is willing and capable of taking care of the child, then the child is placed in a foster home until the hearing. The first hearing at juvenile court must take place within forty-eight hours. By that time, CPS has designated a social worker to present the case to the juvenile court and a petition is filed to have the child declared a dependent child of the court. The first hearing in juvenile court is termed a detention hearing. At this time, the court determines whether the child should remain in the home or be detained out of the home. The parents are each entitled to appointed counsel and the juvenile court appoints an attorney to represent the child.

Grandparents may be allowed to participate in this hearing as, "The court may nevertheless admit any person it deems to have a direct and legitimate interest in the particular case." The statutes go further and state in Rule 1412(e) . . . "Upon a sufficient showing, the court may recognize the child's present or previous custodians as de facto parents and grant standing to participate as parties in disposition hearings and any hearing thereafter at which the status of the dependent child is at issue.

The de facto parent may:
(1)   Be present at the hearing;
(2)   Be represented by retained counsel, or at the discretion of the court, by appointed counsel; and
(3)   Present evidence."

The best advice for grandparents is to be involved in the juvenile court process AS SOON AS POSSIBLE to obtain standing to participate in the proceedings as grandparents are given preferential placement. By not participating right away, the grandparents may be deemed as having waived their rights to placement. Some grandparents may have de facto parent status. A "de facto parent" is a person who has been found by the court to have assumed, on a day-to-day basis, the role of the parent, fulfilling both the child's physical and psychological needs for care and affection, and who has assumed that role for a substantial period of time.

If you learn your grandchild is within the jurisdiction of the juvenile court, contact the Department of Social Services right away and make contact with the social worker in charge of the case. Even without a court appearance, visitations can be arranged and placement can be changed. The longer the grandparent waits to be involved in the juvenile court proceedings, the more difficult it is to change placement.

If the social worker does not cooperate to allow the grandparents access to the grandchild or placement of the child, the grandparent has the right to ask the court for intervention. This request (termed a 388 petition) is to be filled out by the grandparents at the juvenile court clerk's office. A court date is then assigned for the grandparents to directly request placement from the judge. A copy of Welfare and Institutions Code Section 388 is found at the back of this book.

After a finding at the disposition hearing that the child is in need of court supervision, the court will put a plan in effect to reunite the parents with the child. A further hearing is scheduled to review the case. If the parents have complied with the requirements of reunification, then the matter is dismissed at the review hearing. Once the case is dismissed, the child is returned to the parents and the court's intervention is terminated.

If the parents do not comply with the reunification plan, the probation officer and social worker for the child commence proceedings to free the child for adoption. The child is placed in a preadopt home. A petition to terminate the rights of the parents may be filed and a trial held on the ability of the parents to be reunited with the child.

The preadopt family consists of parents who have been approved for adoption and have been waiting for a child to adopt. Once the child is placed in a preadopt home, it is assumed that the child will be adopted by the family when the rights of the parents are terminated. This process takes as little as twelve months, but the court can grant an extension up to eighteen months from the original removal. If the child is adopted by a non-relative after the child is freed for adoption, the grandparents have no further rights to visitations.

Grandparents can be preadopt parents and can adopt the grandchild in the same manner as non-relative preadopt parents.

Chapter Five

ADOPTION

Once a child has been adopted by a non-relative, visitation rights by relatives are terminated. Even if the grandparent had visitation in a family law action, those rights would be extinguished with the granting of an adoption petition.

KINSHIP ADOPTION

The one exception to this rule is called a kinship adoption. This type of adoption can occur during a normal adoption procedure and it can also occur when a child is found to be, or is likely to be, a dependent of the juvenile court. Along with the petition to adopt the child filed by a relative, the parents and other relatives can file a kinship adoption agreement. The agreement permits continuing contact between the birth relatives and the child. The underlying test is whether or not the contact is in the child's best interest.

The agreement can be modified, enforced or terminated by the court which granted the adoption.

A copy of Family Code Sections 8714.5, 8714.7, 8715, and 8802 can be found at the end of this book which more fully describes relative and kinship adoptions.

Chapter Six

FEES

Each county charges different fees for different activities within the court system. The following is an overview of the fees that may be charged. Contact your county clerk to determine the actual fees charged by your county. At this writing, fees may not be charged for mediation. The filing fee for a petition is $185. The filing fee for a motion is $23. Process servers usually charge $25 for each document served if it is within the city limits. It will be more for out of area service and hard to locate service.

1. Independent Lawsuit	Filing fee for an initial petition
	Filing fee for papers to obtain a court date
	Additional fees for investigators
2. Joinder	Filing fee for motion to request joinder
	Filing fee for petition after joinder
	Filing fee for papers to obtain a court date
	Additional fees for investigators
3. Guardianship	Filing fee for petition for guardianship
	Court investigation fee
	Filing fee for subsequent motions to change visitation
4. Dependency actions	No filing fee for requesting a court date
5. Adoption	No filing fee if filed in Juvenile Court
6. Attorney Fees	There is a provision in the Family Code which allows for the court to make any party pay attorney fees to the other parties. This is usually based on the needs of the parties requesting fees and the ability of the other party to pay the fees.
7. Child Support	Family Code 3103 allows for the grandparents to participate in the cost of visitation for transportation, provision of basic medical expenses, daycare costs, other necessities.

Chapter Seven

ADVICE FROM THE AUTHOR

There are a few cases that require special consideration and explanation. Although these issues are dealt with primarily in association with the parents, they do come up in grandparent visitation and guardianship cases.

UNUSUAL CIRCUMSTANCES

Child Sexual Abuse

In cases where there are allegations of child sexual abuse, the outcome of mediation is the alleged molester is given short frequent contact with the child, but the contact is supervised. The mediators frequently encourage the parents to agree to a mutual supervisor.

If it is not possible to agree on a supervisor, the mediator may recommend that a supervisor be provided by a local group which treats molest victims and their parents. There is usually an hourly fee. An investigation may be ordered as well. The investigator will review the police reports, talk with the molested victim, gather information from mental health professionals who have treated the child and file a report with the court.

The return to court date is usually ninety days away in order to allow the time necessary for the investigator to complete the report. The investigator who will conduct the investigation is usually appointed by the judge. There is frequently a charge for the investigation.

The investigation report may include a recommendation to the court on future plans for contact between the child and the accused parent. This will frequently include continued contact with a supervisor present and an order that the offender attend counseling. Sometimes counseling with the accused and the child together is recommended. During the ninety-day period, the contact will usually remain frequent with supervision.

Physical Abuse of Child

The pattern in mediation is very similar to the one for child sexual abuse. Contact is usually allowed between the accused and the child, but in the presence of a supervisor to keep the child safe.

Mental Abuse

There may be an allegation of mental or emotional abuse of the child. These situations are generally dealt with by restraining orders regarding discussing the litigation or other sensitive areas with the child or in the presence of the child. Parties should avoid entering into discussions with the child about what the other parties do or if the other parties have a new "friend."

Alcohol or Drug Abuse

In most instances, these allegations are the subject of restraining orders. The typical language of the restraining order is found at the end of chapter three. In extreme cases, the visitation may be conditioned on the requirement that the alleged alcohol or drug abuser be participating in some acceptable form of rehabilitation treatment with letters of successful participation being a requirement of ongoing contact.

Some mediators will recommend that a party can request random drug tests of the party believed to have a drug problem. The requesting party pays for the test in advance. There may or may not be restrictions on the number of tests that can be ordered or the frequency with which the tests can be requested.

In cases where you are requesting an extreme remedy, the mediator will usually require that you provide objective evidence such as drunk driving convictions, evidence of alcohol related crimes or accidents, conviction for sales or possession of drugs. Just saying the other party has a drinking or drug problem without objective evidence will most likely result in the issuance of a restraining order, but not more.

Absent Parent or Parent who has Not Exercised Visitation for a Long Period of Time

In the case where there has been no visitation for a long period of time (six months or more), the usual plan for visitation includes a period of <u>reunification</u>. This means that the visitation will begin to occur in short, frequent intervals and build up to longer intervals later. The purpose is to give the child a chance to adjust to the visitation gradually without being thrown into an extended plan that may have some adverse effect on them.

EXCHANGE ISSUES

The mediators usually suggest <u>shared transportation</u>. In many cases, shared transportation will work out fine. However, if you are ordered to deliver the child a long distance away when you have clearly stated that your car has broken down and you are taking the bus to and from work, you have a problem. Most mediators will attempt to get an agreement on shared transportation. If shared transportation will create potential problems, negotiate the transportation issue during mediation. If you absolutely cannot share in the transportation, be prepared to discuss alternatives, such as buses, trains or planes. If there is no agreement, the judge will decide the issue. Sometimes the judge will order shared transportation only if child support is current.

It is also common where there are extreme and open hostilities between the parties to have the exchange of the child occur in a public place rather than the home of either parent. Other variations of the theme may be specific orders:

- The receiving party cannot get out of the vehicle during the exchange of the child.

- The sending party cannot go out of the front door during the exchange of the minor child.

- The receiving party may not enter the gate of the sending parent's residence.

- A mutually acceptable third person will be available to observe during the exchange of the child.

- Sometimes the best arrangement is an exchange at the local police department.

Some parties use the exchange as an opportunity to be verbally abusive. One suggestion is to wear a tape recorder. As soon as the contact is made with the other party, make the statement that all conversations between the parties are being tape recorded. This will usually stop abusive tirades. The use of a tape recorder also has the effect of putting the other party on notice that you intend to be on your best behavior as well. Small tape recorders are cheap and can fit inside your pocket.

Another transportation issue is whether anyone except the parties should be allowed to pick up and deliver the grandchild. This issue frequently comes up <u>after</u> mediation, but should be anticipated and addressed <u>during</u> the mediation process.

It's disturbing to have a strange person show up at your door and say the other party could not make it, and they are there to get the grandchild for the visitation. It may also be annoying to have the other grandparents or other family members always picking up and delivering the grandchild.

The questions arise about who is really getting the visitation and why isn't the other party available. Ask the mediator to address specifically the question of who will pick up or deliver the grandchild so there will be a clear understanding before it becomes a problem.

OTHER PROBLEM AREAS

Many questions arise during the course of raising children within the context of the broken home that have given rise to "conventional wisdom" and also create stress. The following are answers to some of the ongoing kinds of questions you might encounter. They will give you some insight into how the courts and the family court services deal with them.

Q.   At what age can a child choose which parent he or she wants to live with?

A.   The legal answer is never. California does not have a given age at which time a child's decision is the determining factor in deciding custody. The older the child, the more weight is to be given to their preference. The court is to evaluate the maturity of the child and the reasoning behind the preference.

Q.   Each time my grandchild comes to visit, he or she begs to come live with me. What do I tell him or her?

A.   Children very often feel a need to express their love for their parent and grandparents and their commitment to the relationship. Frequently this takes the form of asking to live with the non-custodial parent or grandparent. Sometimes the need to tell the grandparent they want to live with them comes from the loyalty conflict that the grandchild feels when one or the other parent is putting the grandchild under pressure to "choose" the custodial parent.

Remember, <u>where the grandchild lives is a parenting decision.</u> If the parents cannot agree, then it becomes a decision of the court. The court will not change custody based on the grandchild's preference <u>alone</u> when strong evidence is absent that the current custodial environment is detrimental to the grandchild.

Tell your grandchild how much you would love him or her to come and live with you, but it is really up to the adults to determine what is best for the grandchild and right now they have decided the current arrangement is best.

Q.   I am the custodial grandparent. Every time I send my grandchild to visit with their mother/father, they never bring back the clothes that I sent.

A.   This is a common problem and the answer is simple. Buy additional clothing for the grandchild according to the seasons and give the extra clothing to the non-custodial parents.

For example, if the grandchild is spending alternate weekends, then the non-custodial parents will need two complete sets of outerwear, two sets of underwear, socks and shoes. In the summertime, they should be given a swimsuit and thongs.

In the wintertime, they should be given an extra jacket and sweater. Give the clothes to the non-custodial parents and tell him or her that these clothes are for the grandchild when the grandchild is with him or her, <u>and</u> that you expect the grandchild to be returned in the same clothing that they arrive in for the visitation. Also explain this to the grandchild so that they know they are to return in the clothes they were wearing when they were sent. The clothes that you give to the non-custodial parents are not to be returned. You should buy according to the seasons. If the grandchild is going to visit for more than one week at a time, send along six or seven nonreturnable outfits.

The clothing may be purchased at garage sales, consignment shops or other thrift shops so that the financial investment is minimum compared to the peace of mind of not dealing with the same issue after each visitation.

Q.   Every time I call to talk to my grandchild when he or she is with the father/mother, I never get through. They say he or she is out playing or has already gone to bed.

A.   Deal with this issue in mediation. It is appropriate to get an order for reasonable telephone access to include specific hours of the day or days of the week for contact with the non-custodial party.

Q.   Every time I go to get my grandchild for visitation, my daughter-in-law/son-in-law uses this as a time to get in my face about whatever is ailing her or him that day.

A.   There can be restraining orders regarding the conduct of the parties <u>during</u> the exchange of the grandchild. One remedy is to wear a tape recorder with the microphone showing <u>and</u> state immediately upon encountering the parent that the conversation is being recorded.

The use of the tape recorder will also help you monitor your reactions to the assaults of the mother or father of the grandchild. Use the same practice when the other party uses the telephone contact as a screaming match. As soon as you answer and realize who it is, state immediately that the conversation is being recorded.

Q.   My ex-daughter-in-law's new husband/ex-son-in-law's new wife keeps butting in during the conversations regarding the grandchild. He or she won't make him or her shut up, and I am getting short-fused over the situation.

A.   In mediation, request that only the parents be present during the transfer of the grandchild. Also request that <u>only</u> the parents discuss the custody issues regarding the grandchild and each party will not allow a third person to interfere.

You can also file civil harassment lawsuits against the new spouse directly to bring them within the jurisdiction of the court and subject to a restraining order.

Q.   I am the custodial grandparent. My grandchild keeps telling me they don't want to go to visit their mother/father. What can I do?

A.   Legally, you must make the grandchild available for visitation with the non-custodial parents if there is a visitation order in place. The approach will vary depending on the age of the grandchild. One approach is to make sure the grandchild is in the house and personally escort the grandchild to the front door when the non-custodial parent arrives. Stay out of the conversation between the non-custodial parent and the grandchild. Walk away a short distance.

Grandchildren very often feel they must be loyal to the custodial grandparent and they show their loyalty by showing some open rejection of the non-custodial parents. Interestingly enough, when cases are taken to trial where one of the issues is the grandchild's reluctance to go for visitation, it seems there is always a witness who saw the grandchild shortly after they were picked up for visitation. The witness talks about how wonderfully happy the grandchild seemed and how closely bonded they appeared to be with their visiting parent.

If the problem becomes one where there are physical symptoms around the visitation issue, take the grandchild to a therapist who will usually get the visiting parents involved in therapy and get to the root of the problem.

When the grandchild is older, the problem is harder. Do the same thing as with the young grandchild. Make sure they are at home and at the front door. If the grandchild is absolutely adamant about not going for visitation, the issue is between the grandchild and the other parent - not you and the other parent. Let them work it out and stay out of it.

Q.   I am the custodial grandparent. My grandchild is sick sometimes when it is the mother/father's visitation. How sick does he or she have to be to keep them here?

A.   You and the parents of the grandchild know the grandchild better than anyone else. You know whether your grandchild runs a temperature easily or not at all. You also know when the illness is serious and cause for concern and anxiety.

Discuss this in mediation if you anticipate a problem. Some parents have agreed that the grandchild would not go to visitation if the temperature was more than 101 degrees.

Other parents have decided to address it on a case-by-case basis with the non-custodial parents having an opportunity to see and talk with the grandchild and then reach a decision as to what would be in the grandchild's best interest at that time. Other parents have felt that their commitment to parenting included taking care of the grandchild during the hard times as well as the good times and believe taking the grandchild for visitation when he or she is ill is completely appropriate.

If there is a court order for visitation, you must allow the visitation to occur unless your doctor gives you a note that says the grandchild is not to be removed from your residence.

Q.   Getting an agreement is wonderful, but I know they will not live up to it. They have refused to cooperate before. What remedies do I have if they don't return the grandchild?

A.   First of all, visitation is the non-custodial parent's right to access, <u>not</u> your grandchild's right to see the other parent. If the parents do not show up for visitation, the only option you have is to bring the matter back to court to have the visitation restricted so that you are not in a position of having to be available every other weekend when there is no pattern of visitation.

If you do not get your visitation, the remedy is to file a contempt of court proceeding charging the custodial party with contempt of the order of the court. This is a quasi-criminal proceeding and the possible outcomes are probation, a jail sentence, a large fine or all of the above. You can also call the police department. The police officers will frequently call the violating parent and demand compliance with the court order. Have a copy of the visitation order to review with the police.

Q.   My ex-daughter-in-law/ex-son-in-law's parenting skills are lousy. She or he always keeps the grandchild upset. What can be done?

A.   Many counties have an office that offers a free class on parenting skills. Ask your mediator for a referral. There are also programs offered in most communities.

Q.   I think the mediator does not listen to me and is prejudiced against me. Can I get another mediator?

A.   There is a procedure for complaints against a mediator. If you feel the mediator is unfair or prejudiced against you, ask for information on the county's procedure to handle complaints about mediators. A complaint process is required by statute.

HELPFUL HINTS

Some of this information may seem very simple and may offend you. Some of it may not be pertinent to you personally. These recommendations are based on observation of many clients and of opposing party's conduct.

These are the recommendations for practical and good etiquette in a court mediation setting. Remember, the mediators are skillful in "reading" people, and it is important that you seem warm and sincere.

1.   Wear appropriate clothing to court. Appropriate is defined as what you would wear to church or a social daytime gathering. Shorts are inappropriate.

2.   Be prepared to answer questions with short answers. If the mediator is attempting to get a "fix" on your prior relationship with the grandchild, he or she may ask a series of questions. Answer them *directly*. Remember, they are asking you for the time of day, not how to build a clock.

     Be honest in your answers, but not to the extent that you bare your soul of all of the sins you have committed. Save that for confession. The only issue is what is best for your grandchild, not how sorry you are that your son's or daughter's relationship has broken up.

3.   Do not speak directly to either parent. Sometimes in mediation, the parent who is opposing your request for visitation may know you so intimately they know what to say to "get your goat." Of course, they also want to make you look bad in front of the mediator.

It may be difficult for you to sit there and listen to the lies that are being told about you, but you will be given a chance to tell the truth and set the record straight. Bring a notebook with you. If there are distortions of importance, make a note to yourself and when it is your turn, you can tell the real story.

4.   Don't get hung up on trivia. With all of the emotion that you are feeling, it will be easy to be distracted with trivia. Trivia is defined as the unimportant things that have absolutely no significance.

Example: If the parent opposing your request for visitation says you have a drinking problem because you came over to the house one time smelling like beer, mention that you had just left the company picnic.

Address the issue head-on. Addressing the issue head-on shows the mediator you are honest and are not attempting to hide anything significant, such as a drinking problem.

5.   Do not speak directly to or respond to questions from either parent's attorney. Some attorneys like to "posture" in front of their client to show how "tough" they are by being rude or offensive to you. Do not respond. The other attorney is being paid to do a job. Your main concern is to keep the focus of the mediation on the best interests of your grandchild.

6.   Make eye contact with the mediator. Non-verbal communication is very important for one reason; space in the mediation room may be rather small and all physical movement, even slight, has an impact.

Keep your hand away from your mouth when you talk. Speak up so that everyone can hear what you are saying. Don't be afraid to be assertive, yet not aggressive, in discussing your grandchild's need to have an ongoing relationship with you.

7.   Do not take reams of papers or records in and expect the mediator to read them. A concise summary may be appropriate. The mediators like to hear your story instead of reading about it.

8.   Do not take in cassettes. If you have recorded information on a cassette of either the other parent or your grandchild, you should have the cassette transcribed. On the transcriptions, highlight the areas you want to draw to the mediator's attention.

Even before any court orders are made, it is important that you understand how to facilitate obtaining and implementing visitations. This advice is based on conversations with therapists, mediators and the author's personal experience as a Family Law Specialist and as a grandmother.

It is best for you not to get involved in the parents' marital disputes. Try to remain neutral for the benefit of the grandchild. Do not make disparaging comments about either parent when the grandchild is with you. Remember, the grandchild is one-half of each parent. Rejection of one of the grandchild's parents is also a rejection of part of the grandchild.

The best advice is to keep the grandchild's feelings as the most important issue. Recognize that by saying negative comments to the grandchild about a parent is hurtful to the grandchild. The best thing you can give your grandchild is unqualified love and acceptance. This may be shown by giving the grandchild's parents unqualified love and acceptance.

Chapter Eight

ABOUT THE AUTHOR

E. F. Cash-Dudley, known to her friends and clients as "Eddy" was born and raised in the San Joaquin Valley. She was a "re-entry" woman at Merced Community College and graduated with honors in 1976. She was the valedictorian of her graduating class.

In 1979, she graduated from California State University, Stanislaus with a Bachelor's Degree in Communication Studies. She graduated from the University of California, Hastings College of the Law in 1982 and begun practicing family law in Modesto, California.

Eddy took the examination for certification as a family law specialist in 1986. In February 1988, she was certified as a family law specialist by the California State Bar Board of Legal Certification. Eddy is married to an Animal Nutritionist/Entrepreneur, has three children and two grandchildren. Other publications include <u>Tips On Child Custody Mediation In Stanislaus County.</u>

CAREGIVER'S AUTHORIZATION AFFIDAVIT

Use of this affidavit is authorized by Part 1.5 (commencing with Section 6550) of Division 11 of the California Family Code. Instructions: Completion of items 1-4 and the signing of the affidavit is sufficient to authorize enrollment of a minor in school and authorize school-related medical care. Completion of items 5-8 is additionally required to authorize any other medical care. Print clearly.

The minor named below lives in my home and I am 18 years of age or older.

1. Name of Minor

_____

2. Minor's date of birth _____

3. Name (adult giving authorization)

_____

4. My home address:

_____

_____

_____

5. [ ]   I am a grandparent, aunt, uncle, or other qualified relative of the minor.
          (see back of this form for a definition of "qualified relative").

6.   Check one or both:
          (for example, if one parent was advised and the other cannot be located):

   [ ]   I have advised the parent(s) or other person(s) having legal custody of the minor of my intent to authorize medical care, and have received no objection.

   [ ]   I am unable to contact the parent(s) or other person(s) having legal custody of the minor at this time to notify them of my intended authorization.

7. My date of birth:_____

8. My California driver's license or identification card number_____

WARNING: Do not sign this form if any of the statements above are incorrect, or you will be committing a crime punishable by a fine, imprisonment, or both.

I declare under penalty of perjury under the laws of the State of California that the foregoing is true and correct.

Dated:_____   Signed:_____

NOTICES:

1. This declaration does not affect the rights of the minor's parents or legal guardian regarding the care, custody, and control of the minor, and does not mean that the caregiver has legal custody of the minor.

2. A person who relies on this affidavit has no obligation to make any further inquiry or investigation.

3. This affidavit is not valid for more than one year after the date on which it is executed.

Additional Information:

TO CAREGIVERS:

1. "Qualified relative", for purposes of item 5, means a spouse, parent, stepparent, brother, sister, stepbrother, stepsister, half-brother, half-sister, uncle, aunt, niece, nephew, first cousin, or any person denoted by the prefix "grand" or "great", or the spouse of any of the persons specified in this definition, even after the marriage has been terminated by death or dissolution.

2. The law may require you, if you are not a relative or a currently licensed foster parent, to obtain a foster home license in order to care for a minor. If you have any questions, please contact your local department of social services.

3. If the minor stops living with you, you are required to notify any school, health care provider, or health care service plan to which you have given this affidavit.

4. If you do not have the information requested in item 9 (California driver's license or I.D.), provide another form of identification such as your social security number or Medi-Cal number.

TO SCHOOL OFFICIALS:

1. Section 48204 of the Education Code provides that this affidavit constitutes a sufficient basis for a determination of residence of the minor, without the requirement of a guardianship or other custody order, unless the school district determines from actual facts that the minor is not living with the caregiver.

2. The school district may require additional reasonable evidence that the caregiver lives at the address provided in item 4.

TO HEALTH CARE PROVIDERS AND HEALTH CARE SERVICE PLANS:

1. No person who acts in good faith reliance upon a caregiver's authorization affidavit to provide medical or dental care, without actual knowledge of facts contrary to those stated on the affidavit, is subject to criminal liability or to civil liability to any person, or is subject to professional disciplinary action, for such reliance if the applicable portions of the form are completed.

2. This affidavit does not confer dependency for health care coverage purposes.

California County Chart*

The following chart includes important information about the mediation process in each California county.

Name of County: *Lists each county in California alphabetically. Following this chart is a complete list by county with addresses, telephone numbers, parking information, etc.*

Where: *Mediation may be held at the Courthouse or in the community at the Mediator's private office. If mediation is done by the Probation Department or another county office, it may occur in the Courthouse or in the county office.*

Attorney: *Participation by an attorney in the mediation process varies by county.*

Confidential: *If mediation is confidential, then the mediator cannot inform the Judge what was discussed in mediation. If mediation is non-confidential, the mediator can inform the Judge of the reason for the recommendation, or when there is no agreement.*

Recommend: *The mediator can or cannot make a recommendation to the Judge. The Judge may or may not accept.*

*This information was extrapolated from <u>Profile Child Custody Mediation & Evaluation Services in California Superior Courts</u> and personal interviews with the county staff.

Name of County	Where	Attorney		Confidential		Recommend	
		Yes	No	Yes	No	Yes	No
Alameda	Courthouse		X		X	X	
Alpine	Courthouse		X		X	X	
Amador	Private Office		X	X			X
Butte	Courthouse		X	X			X
Calaveras	Courthouse		X		X	X	
Colusa	Courthouse		X		X	X	
Contra Costa	Courthouse		X	X			X
Del Norte	Private Office		X	X			X
El Dorado: Placerville So. Lake Tahoe	Courthouse		X X	X X			X X
Fresno	Courthouse		X		X	X	
Glenn	Courthouse	X			X	X	
Humboldt	Probation Dept.	X			X	X	
Imperial	Probation Dept.		X		X	X	
Inyo	Courthouse		X	X			X

Name of County	Where	Attorney		Confidential		Recommend	
		Yes	No	Yes	No	Yes	No
Kern	Probation Dept.		X	X			X
Kings	Probation Dept.		X		X	X	
Lake	Private Office		X		X	X	
Lassen	Probation Dept.		X		X	X	
Los Angeles	Courthouse	X		X			X
Madera	Courthouse		X		X	X	
Marin	Probation	X		X			X
Mariposa	Courthouse Library		X		X	X	
Mendocino	Courthouse		X		X	X	
Merced	Courthouse		X	X			X
Modoc	Probation Dept.	X		X			X
Mono	Courthouse		X	X			X
Monterey	Probation Dept.		X		X	X	
Napa	Private Office		X	X			X

Name of County	Where	Attorney		Confidential		Recommend	
		Yes	No	Yes	No	Yes	No
Nevada	Probation Dept.		X		X	X	
Orange	Courthouse		X	X			X
Placer	Courthouse		X		X	X	
Plumas	Probation Dept.		X	X			X
Riverside	Courthouse		X		X	X	
San Benito	Courthouse		X		X	X	
San Bernardino	Courthouse		X		X	X	
San Diego	Courthouse		X		X	X	
Sacramento	Courthouse	X			X	X	
San Francisco	Courthouse	X		X			X
San Luis Obispo	Courthouse		X	X			X
San Mateo	Courthouse		X		X	X	
Santa Barbara	Courthouse		X	X			X
Santa Clara	Courthouse		X	X			X

Name of County	Where	Attorney		Confidential		Recommend	
		Yes	No	Yes	No	Yes	No
Santa Cruz	Courthouse		X	X			X
Shasta	Courthouse		X		X	X	
Sierra	Probation Dept.	X			X	X	
Siskiyou	Courthouse		X		X	X	
Solano	Courthouse		X	X			X
Sonoma	Probation Dept.		X		X	X	
Stanislaus	Courthouse	X			X	X	
Sutter	Courthouse		X	X			X
Tehama	Courthouse		X		X	X	
Trinity	Courthouse		X		X	X	
Tulare	Courthouse		X		X	X	
Tuolumne	Probation Dept.		X	X			X
Ventura	Courthouse		X		X	X	
Yolo	Private Of		X		X	X	
Yuba	Courthouse		X	X			X

PERSONAL NOTES :

SURVEY: CALIFORNIA COUNTIES

ALAMEDA COUNTY

1225 Fallon Street #209	24405 Amador Street	5672 Stoneridge Street
Oakland, CA	Hayward, CA	Pleasanton, CA
(510) 272-6070	(510) 670-6344	(510) 551-6883

Alameda County has three courts in Oakland; one in court in Hayward and one in Pleasanton. In <u>Oakland</u>, all papers are to be filed at the main courthouse at 1225 Fallon Street, but hearings on Family Law and Probate are held at 1221 Oak Street. Upon filing of visitation papers, the petitioner is to contact Family Court Services to schedule mediation which is conducted prior to the hearing on the matter. In guardianship cases, the investigation is conducted by the Probate Department court investigator. If mediation is required by the judge, the case will be referred to Family Court Services. Mediation is non-confidential and the mediators <u>do make</u> recommendations to the court. Attorneys are not allowed to participate in mediation. Temporary orders are seldom issued by the Alameda County courts. A pre-mediation orientation is <u>required.</u>

Parking is available in parking lots within one to two blocks with the average cost of $4.50 per day. Metal detectors in use at this time are in the Domestic Violence Court.

ALPINE COUNTY

99 Water Street
Markleeville, CA
(530) 694-2113

All papers will be filed and hearings held at the Alpine County Superior Court. Mediation is required in grandparent visitation and guardianship cases. Hearing dates can be obtained within four (4) weeks. At this writing, pre-mediation orientation is not required. Mediation is non-confidential and the mediators <u>do make</u> recommendations to the judge. Attorneys may be involved in the mediation process if determined to be appropriate by the judge. Mediation services have been contracted with El Dorado County mediation services and mediation occurs in South Lake Tahoe.

Street parking is available within two blocks of the courthouse and it is free. The courthouse is not accessible to the disabled. There are no metal detectors at the present time.

AMADOR COUNTY

108 Court Street
Jackson, CA
(209) 223-6463

All papers are to be filed and hearings held in the Amador County Superior Court. Mediation is confidential and recommendations are not made to the court on the first session. If no agreement, mediators <u>may make</u> recommendations to the court on any subsequent sessions. Participation of attorneys in mediation is not encouraged. It takes thirty (30) to forty-five (45) days to get a hearing date. If the judge orders mediation, the petitioner makes the appointment with the mediator who is a contract mediator. It may also take thirty to forty-five days to see a mediator. A pre-mediation orientation is offered.

Free street parking is available within two blocks of the courthouse. There are no metal detectors at the present time.

BUTTE COUNTY

No. 1 Court Street
Oroville, CA
(530) 538-7551

All papers are filed and hearings held at the Butte County Courthouse. Initial mediation is usually on the hearing date. It is the petitioner's responsibility to schedule mediation after the hearing date is received. Mediation is confidential; mediators <u>do not make</u> recommendations to the court. Attorneys do not participate in mediation. In guardianships, the court investigator is in charge of the grandparent's investigation upon the filing of a petition for guardianship.

There is a free parking lot very close to the court, but it is usually full. Free on-street parking is available within three to four blocks. There are no metal detectors at the present time.

CALAVERAS COUNTY

Government Center
891 Mountain Ranch Road
San Andreas, CA
(209) 754-6311

All papers are to be filed and hearings held in the Calaveras County Superior Court. It is the petitioner's responsibility to schedule a mediation date. It takes about two (2) weeks. It takes four (4) weeks to get an initial hearing date. The mediator is an independent contractor who conducts mediation in their private office. Attorneys do not participate in mediation. Mediation is not confidential and the mediators do make a recommendation at the judge's request, if the parties do not come to an agreement. The court investigator handles guardianship investigations in grandparent guardianship cases.

There are free parking lots at the courthouse. There is a metal detector for use in high-profile cases.

COLUSA COUNTY

547 Market Street
Colusa, CA
(530) 458-0507

All papers are to be filed and hearings held in the Colusa County Superior Court. When the petition is filed, the petitioner makes the appointment for mediation which will take about a week. It takes about four (4) weeks to get a hearing date. Attorneys do not participate in mediation. Mediation is non-confidential and the mediators do make recommendations to the judge when the parties cannot reach an agreement. The Probation Department handles the investigation of grandparent guardianship cases.

Free parking is available in parking lots or on the street within one to two blocks of the courthouse. There is no metal detector at this time.

CONTRA COSTA COUNTY

725 Court Street
Martinez, CA
(510) 646-2950

All papers are filed in the Contra Costa County Superior Court. Cases will be heard in the Family Law Department. Upon filing of the petition, the parties are referred to Family Court Services to schedule a mediation appointment located at 724 Escobar in Martinez. It is possible to set mediation on the same date as the hearing if parties are from out of town; otherwise, mediation should be scheduled before the hearing. It takes about four (4) weeks to get a hearing date and a mediation appointment. Attorneys do not participate in mediation. Mediation is confidential and mediators <u>do not make</u> recommendations to the court. The Probation Department handles the investigation in grandparent guardianship cases.

There are parking lots by the courthouse, but are usually full of staff and jurors. On-street parking is available in residential neighborhoods two to three blocks away. There is no metal detector at this time.

DEL NORTE COUNTY

450 "H" Street
Crescent City, CA
(707) 464-7205

All papers are filed and hearings held in the Del Norte Superior Court. To get mediation, the parties must contact the mediator for an appointment. This could take a month since there is only one mediator and only a few appointments available each week. A hearing date can be obtained in about one month and placed on the Law & Motion Calendar on Fridays at 9:00 a.m. Attorneys do not participate in mediation. Mediation is confidential and mediators <u>do make</u> recommendations to the court. The Probation Department handles the investigation in grandparent guardianship cases.
There is free parking in parking lots and on the street within one block. The court does have a metal detector.

EL DORADO COUNTY

495 Main Street
Placerville, CA
(530) 621-6426

The superior court clerk at El Dorado County indicated that El Dorado County has one superior court. However, according to the information received from the Statewide Offices of Family Court Services, there is also a superior court branch in South Lake Tahoe. All papers are to be filed and hearings held at either of these two locations. After the papers are filed requesting grandparent visitations, the petitioner makes an appointment with the mediator. It will take two (2) to three (3) weeks to get an appointment. It takes twenty (20) to twenty-five (25) days to get a hearing date. Attorneys are not involved in mediation. All mediation is confidential. Generally the mediators do not make recommendations. The exception is that mediators can make recommendations in chambers at settlement conferences with the parents. The Probation Department handles the investigation in grandparent guardianship cases.

Parking is at a premium in Placerville. There are parking lots available adjacent to the courthouse at $.50 per hour, but are usually full. On-street parking is available within two to three blocks with a two-hour limit and is closely monitored. There is a metal detector in the courthouse.

FRESNO COUNTY

1100 Van Ness #401
Fresno, CA
(209) 488-1825

All papers are to be filed in the Fresno County Superior Court. Hearings are held in the Family Law Department. Guardianship hearings are conducted in the Probate Department. When the petition for grandparent visitation is filed, the parties are advised by the clerk to contact Family Court Services for a mediation appointment. A pre-mediation orientation is offered. Both the appointment and hearing date are set approximately six (6) weeks away. It is possible to have mediation on the same date as the hearing. Attorneys do not participate in mediation. Mediation is non-confidential and the mediators do make recommendations to the judge. In grandparent guardianship cases, the investigation is handled by the Probate Investigator.

There are parking lots within two blocks of the courthouse at an average cost of $7.00 per day. Street parking is metered. Parking is available at $1.00 per day six to ten blocks away. The courthouse does have a metal detector.

GLENN COUNTY

526 West Sycamore Street
Willows, CA
(916) 934-6407

All papers are to be filed and hearings are held at Glenn County Superior Court. When the petition is filed for grandparent visitation, the clerk assigns two court dates. Both hearing dates and mediation dates are available within three (3) weeks. All that is needed is time to serve papers and be within the time limits set by law. It is possible to have mediation on the same day as the hearing, but this seldom happens. Attorneys may attend the mediation meeting. Mediation is not confidential and the mediators do make recommendations to the judge. In grandparent guardianship cases, the investigation is usually done by the Court Investigator. If the child is under age six (6), the case is referred to Social Services.

On-street parking is available within two blocks of the courthouse at no charge. There is no metal detector at the present time.

HUMBOLDT COUNTY

825 - 5th Street
Eureka, CA
(707) 269-1200

All papers are to be filed in the Humboldt County Superior Court. Hearings are held in the Family Law Department for grandparent visitation and in the Probate Division for guardianship cases. The court sets the appointment for mediation. It takes one (1) to three (3) weeks to get an appointment for mediation. Attorneys may be present in mediation if the client chooses. Mediation is not confidential and mediators do make recommendations to the court. The Probation Department handles the investigation in grandparent guardianship cases.

Free parking is available within two blocks of the courthouse. There is no metal detector at this time.

IMPERIAL COUNTY

939 West Main Street
El Centro, CA
(619) 339-4217

All papers are to be filed at the Imperial County Superior Court. Hearings are held in the Family Law Department for grandparent visitation cases and the Probate Department for guardianship cases. It takes two (2) to three (3) weeks to get a hearing date and about the same length of time to set a mediation appointment. The petitioner sets the mediation appointment. Cases are set on the Law & Motion Calendar at 8:30 a.m. on Wednesdays. Attorneys are not involved in the mediation process. All mediation is non-confidential, but the judge may ask for recommendations. The Probation Department handles grandparent guardianship investigations only if ordered by the judge.

There are two free parking lots across the street from the courthouse. There is no metal detector in the courthouse at this time, but can have one available if needed.

INYO COUNTY

168 N. Edwards Street
Independence, CA
(760) 878-0218

Inyo County has one Superior Court where all papers are to be filed and all hearings held. The grandparent who files for visitation is given a list of mediators and sets their own appointment. The time it takes to get an appointment varies by mediator. Petitioners may set their own hearing date (clear it with the clerk) on the Law & Motion Calendar on the first and third Fridays at 1:30 p.m. Attorneys do not usually participate in mediation. The mediation is confidential and mediators do not make recommendations to the court. Grandparent guardianships may be handled by the Probation Department, but it is more likely that the judge would appoint a private party to conduct the investigation.

Parking is readily available within one block of the courthouse and it is free; in fact, you can probably get a spot right in front of the courthouse. There is no metal detector in the courthouse at this time.

KERN COUNTY

1415 Truxtun Avenue
Bakersfield, CA
(805) 861-5393

All papers are to be filed at the Kern County Superior Court. Hearings are held in the Family Law Department for grandparent visitation cases and the Probate Department for guardianship cases. The petitioning grandparent is to set their own appointment with the mediator which is usually within three (3) weeks. The hearing date should be set with the clerk at least three weeks away to allow for service and mediation. A pre-mediation orientation is offered. Attorneys do not participate in mediation. Mediation is confidential. If there is an agreement, the mediator states only terms of the agreement to the court. In grandparent guardianship matters, the investigation is handled by Family Court Services.

There is a free parking lot across the street from the courthouse with a two-hour limit. Street parking is only 36 minutes and is strictly enforced. There is a parking lot on L Street (approximately two blocks) that offers free parking all day. There is a metal detector in the courthouse.

KINGS COUNTY

1400 W. Lacey Boulevard
Hanford, CA
(209) 582-3211

All papers are to be filed in the Kings County Superior Court. Hearings are held in the Family Law Department for grandparent visitation cases and the Probate Department for guardianship cases. Mediation is handled by the Probation Department. When mediation is requested, clerks refer to the Probation Department with a referral sheet and the parties make their own appointments. It takes about eight (8) weeks to get an appointment. A pre-mediation orientation is offered. Attorneys do not participate in mediation. The mediation session is non-confidential and the mediators do make recommendations to the judge. Grandparent guardianship investigations are also handled by the Probation Department.

Free parking is available in parking lots and on the street within two blocks of the courthouse. A wand-type metal detector is used by the bailiffs.

LAKE COUNTY

255 North Forbes Street
Lakeport, CA
(707) 263-2274

All papers are to be filed and all hearings are held in the Lake County Courthouse. Lake County has two Superior Courts; there are no separate divisions for Family Law or Probate. The petitioning grandparent sets their own appointment with the mediator, usually within two (2) weeks. Hearings can be set on the Law & Motion Calendar on Mondays at 9:00 a.m. In setting the date, allow time for mediation and service of papers. Attorneys are not involved in the mediation process. Mediation is non-confidential and the mediators do make recommendations to the judge if requested. The Probation Department handles the investigation in grandparent guardianship cases.

There is a parking lot behind the courthouse and plenty of on-street parking within one block. There is no charge for parking. There is a metal detector in the courthouse.

LASSEN COUNTY

220 S. Lassen Street
Susanville, CA
(916) 251-8189

All papers are to be filed and hearings are held at the Lassen County Superior Court. If mediation has not occurred prior to the hearing date, the judge will order the parties to mediation and continue the hearing. The petitioner is to complete the packet of forms and set the appointment. Appointments are set in the order the completed forms are received. Mediation is handled by the Probation Department. Mediation is not confidential and the mediators do make recommendations to the judge. Attorneys do not usually participate in mediation. A pre-mediation orientation is required. The Probation Department handles the investigation in grandparent guardianship cases.

Parking is readily available at no charge within one block of the courthouse. There is no metal detector in the courthouse at the present time.

LOS ANGELES COUNTY

Central District
111 N. Hill Street
Los Angeles, CA
(213) 974-1234

East District
400 Civic Center Plaza
Pomona, CA
(909) 620-3023

North Central District
300 E. Olive Avenue
Burbank, CA
(818) 557-3482

North Central District
600 E. Broadway
Glendale, CA
(818) 500-3551

Northeast District
300 E. Walnut St.
Pasadena, CA
(626) 356-5689

North Valley District
900 Third Street
San Fernando, CA
(818) 374-2659

North District
1040 W. Avenue "J" #122
Lancaster, CA
(805) 945-6477

Northwest District
6230 Sylmar Avenue
Van Nuys, CA
(818) 374-2208

South District
415 W. Ocean Blvd.
Long Beach, CA
(562) 491-5929

Catalina
215 Summer Avenue
Avalon, CA
(310) 510-0026

South Central District
200 W. Compton Blvd.
Compton, CA
(310) 603-7842

Southeast District
12720 Norwalk Blvd.
Norwalk, CA
(310) 807-7261

Southwest District
825 Maple Avenue
Torrance, CA
(310) 222-8808

West District
1725 Main Street
Santa Monica, CA
(310) 260-3616

Los Angeles County has fourteen (14) districts. In the larger districts, there are Family Law and Probate Divisions. It is recommended to telephone for further information from the specific district when ready to file papers.

Mediation is required prior to the hearing. The petitioner is to schedule mediation which takes place in three (3) to five (5) weeks. The hearing should be set to allow time for mediation and service. Attorneys are included in the first ten (10) or so minutes of mediation in a general discussion; attorneys also participate when an agreement is reached to make sure their clients understand the agreement. Mediation is confidential and mediators do not make recommendations to the court. A pre-mediation orientation is offered in at least three (3) of the districts. In grandparent guardianship cases, the investigation is handled by the Probate Department Court Investigator.

Most districts have free parking for the public within two blocks of the courthouse. The Central District has parking lots within two to three blocks that cost $8.00 to $12.00 per day. Some courts have metal detectors.

MADERA COUNTY

209 W. Yosemite Avenue
Madera, CA
(209) 675-7907

All papers are to be filed and hearings held in the Madera County Superior Court. The petitioning grandparent is to schedule the mediation appointment; this usually takes one month. The hearing is to be set thirty (30) to forty-five (45) days away to allow for mediation and service. A pre-mediation video orientation is offered. Attorneys are not involved in the mediation process. Mediation is non-confidential and mediators <u>do make</u> recommendations to the judge. Grandparent guardianship investigations are handled by Family Court Services.

Free on-street parking is available within two blocks of the courthouse. A metal detector may be used at the entrance to courtrooms.

MARIN COUNTY

3501 Civic Center Drive
San Rafael, CA
(415) 499-6244

All papers are to be filed and hearings held in the Marin County Superior Court. A pre-mediation orientation is required and takes place on Thursdays at 11:00 a.m. The mediator will contact the parties by letter after the orientation to schedule an appointment. This will take about three (3) weeks. Hearings should be set by the Law & Motion clerk at least one (1) month away to allow for mediation and service. Attorneys and clients are directed to meet and confer on unresolved issues. Mediation is confidential and mediators <u>do not make</u> recommendations to the court. Court investigators handle the investigation in grandparent guardianship cases.

Free parking is available around the courthouse building with a two-hour time limit. Metal detectors are available in some courtrooms.

MARIPOSA COUNTY

5088 Bullion Street
Mariposa, CA
(209) 966-2005

All papers are to be filed and hearings held in the Mariposa County Superior Court. It takes about three (3) weeks to get an appointment for mediation and this is set by the court as the mediator is from Merced County. The clerk sets the hearing on a mediation date, usually on the first or third Monday of the month. A pre-mediation orientation is offered. Attorneys are not involved in mediation. Mediation is non-confidential and mediators do make recommendations to the judge. The Probation Department handles the investigation in grandparent guardianship cases.

Free on-street parking is available around the courthouse, from one to three blocks away. Hand-held metal detectors are in use as necessary.

MENDOCINO COUNTY

State & Perkins Streets
Ukiah, CA
(707) 463-4664

All papers are filed and hearings held in the Mendocino County Superior Court. Mediation is set on the same day as the hearing. When papers are filed, the clerk will set this date about four (4) weeks away. Attorneys do not participate in mediation. Mediation is non-confidential and mediators do make recommendations to the court. Child Protective Services handle the investigation in grandparent guardianship cases.

Parking lots are for permit parking only and street parking is limited to one and one-half hours. Space is limited and you may go several blocks to find a space. Metal detectors are in use in the courthouse.

MERCED COUNTY

670 W. 21st Street
Merced, CA
(209) 385-7531

All papers are to be filed and hearings held in the Merced County Superior Court. Merced has a family law court behind the Merced mall, but it does not handle mediation cases at this time. Appointments are made for mediation at the time of filing. The hearing is set twenty (20) to twenty-five (25) days away to allow for mediation one week before the hearing. A pre-mediation video orientation is offered. Mediation is scheduled two (2) days per week and cases are assigned by court case number (even/odd). Attorneys do not participate in mediation. Mediation is confidential and mediators <u>do not make</u> recommendations to the court. In grandparent guardianship cases, the investigation is handled by court investigators.

There is a free parking lot across the street from the courthouse and free on-street parking within three blocks. There is no metal detector in use at the present time.

MODOC COUNTY

205 S. East Street
Alturas, CA
(916) 233-6222

All papers are to be filed and hearings held in the Modoc County Superior Court. Mediation cases can be set on the hearing date or before the hearing. If set before, it takes two (2) to four (4) weeks to get an appointment. Hearings are set at least fifteen (15) days out to allow for service. It is not usual, but attorneys can be involved in mediation. The mediation process is confidential and mediators <u>do not make</u> recommendations to the court. A pre-mediation orientation is offered. The Probation Department handles the investigation in grandparent guardianship cases.

Free parking lots and on-street parking are available within two blocks of the courthouse. There is no metal detector in use at the present time.

MONO COUNTY

Courthouse, Main Street
Bridgeport, CA
(619) 932-5203

All papers are to be filed and hearings held in the Mono County Superior Court. Mediation can be the same day as the hearing or can be by telephone. Mediators make their own appointments and are quite flexible. The clerk sets the hearing on the Law & Motion calendar on Thursdays. These cases are set within three (3) weeks. If the parties request, attorneys can participate in mediation. Mediation is confidential and the mediators do not make recommendations to the judge. Grandparent guardianship investigations vary. If Child Protective Services already has the case, then they will do the investigation. If there is no case, the investigation would be assigned to mental health professionals from out of the county.

Free parking is available in a small lot and on the street, all within one block of the courthouse. There is no metal detector in use at the present time.

MONTEREY COUNTY

1200 Aguajito Road
Monterey, CA
(408) 647-7730

All papers are to be filed in the Monterey County Superior Court. Hearings are held in the Family Law Department for grandparent visitation and in the Probate Division for guardianship cases. If mediation is requested, the clerk will set a mediation appointment. It takes two (2) to three (3) weeks to get a mediation appointment and four (4) to six (6) weeks to get a hearing on the mediation. Attorneys are not involved in the mediation process. Mediation is non-confidential and mediators do make recommendations to the court. In grandparent guardianship cases, Family Court Services investigators do the investigation.

There are three free parking lots and free on-street parking within two to three blocks of the courthouse. Metal detectors are in use in some courtrooms.

NAPA COUNTY

825 Brown Street
Napa, CA
(707) 253-4481

All papers are to be filed and hearings are held in the Napa County Superior Court. The initial hearing is set by the petitioner for the Law & Motion calendar on Mondays; the date should be cleared with the calendar clerk. If mediation is ordered, the petitioner makes an appointment with the mediator through Family Court Services. This takes three (3) to four (4) weeks. Attorneys are involved only at the request of the client. Mediation is confidential and mediators <u>do not make</u> recommendations to the court. A pre-mediation orientation is required. Family Court investigators complete the investigation in grandparent guardianship matters.

Free public parking lots are available across the street from the courthouse; on-street parking is free and within one to two blocks. Metal detectors are in use in the courthouse.

NEVADA COUNTY

201 Church Street #5
Nevada City, CA
(530) 265-1293

All papers are to be filed and hearings held in the Nevada County Superior Court. Mediation will usually take place on the same day at the first court appearance. A pre-mediation orientation is required. The initial hearing is set by the clerk within three (3) weeks for the Law & Motion calendar, Mondays at 8:30 a.m. and 10:30 a.m. Attorneys do not parti Mediation is non-confidential and the mediators<u> do make</u> recommendations to the court.

There is free parking available on the street by the courthouse, but extremely limited. Metered parking is available within two to three blocks. A portable metal detector may be used in the courthouse.

ORANGE COUNTY

700 Civic Center Drive W.
Santa Ana, CA
(714) 843-3734

All papers are to be filed in the Orange County Superior Court. Hearings are held in the Family Law Department in grandparent visitation cases and the Probate Department for guardianship cases. It takes about four (4) weeks to get an initial hearing. When the request for grandparent visitation is requested in court, the clerk sets the mediation appointment after receiving an intake sheet from the court. A pre-mediation orientation is required. Attorneys do not participate in mediation. Mediation is confidential and mediators do not make recommendations to the court. The exception to this rule is when the mediator recommends an evaluation be completed. There is also voluntary mediation available, even if no papers are filed, if both parents and the grandparents agree to participate. In grandparent guardianship cases, the investigation is handled by either the mediator or court investigator.

Public parking lots are available within one block of the courthouse. Cost is $.75 for twenty minutes, maximum $6.00 to $7.00 per day. Metal detectors are in use in the courthouse.

PLACER COUNTY

101 Maple Street
Auburn, CA
(530) 889-6550

All papers are to be filed in the Placer County Superior Court. Hearings will be held in either the Family Law Department for grandparent visitation cases or the Probate Department for guardianship cases. It takes about a month to get an initial hearing. When the judge orders mediation, parties must first attend a pre-mediation orientation. Appointments for mediation are made at the orientation or by phone. Appointments are usually available within two weeks. Attorneys are not involved in the mediation process. Mediation is non-confidential and the mediators do make recommendations to the court.

Free parking is available in small lots and on the street within one block of the courthouse. Metal detectors are in use in the courthouse.

PLUMAS COUNTY

520 W. Main Street
Quincy, CA
(530) 283-6305

All papers are to filed and hearings held in the Plumas County Superior Court. The parties can request voluntary mediation if all agree. The initial hearing is usually set within four (4) weeks after the petition for grandparent visitation is filed. When mediation is ordered, the petitioner sets an appointment with the mediator, usually in a month. Attorneys do not participate in mediation. Mediation is confidential and the mediators do not make recommendations to the court. In grandparent guardianship cases, the Probation Department handles the investigation.

Free parking is available in lots and on the street within one block of the courthouse. There are no metal detectors in use at the present time.

RIVERSIDE COUNTY

4164 Brockton Avenue
Riverside, CA
(909) 275-1940

4050 Main Street
Riverside, CA
(909) 275-1960

All papers are to be filed and hearings held in the Riverside County Superior Court on Brockton Avenue; guardianships are to be filed and hearings held on Main Street. It takes six (6) weeks to obtain an initial hearing. When papers are filed, the clerk sets the hearing date and a mediation appointment. Attorneys are not involved in the mediation process. The mediation is non-confidential and mediators do make recommendations to the judge. The investigation for grandparent guardianships is handled by the Probation Department.

Brockton Avenue has street parking and it's very difficult to find a spot. A parking lot under the building is reserved for employees and the disabled. All others are ticketed. Parking spaces can be six to eight blocks away. There are no public parking lots. Metal detectors are in use in the courthouse. On Main Street, parking lots are within four blocks and cost $3.00 per day. Street parking is metered and can be found within four blocks. Parking can be very difficult. There are no metal detectors in use at this time.

SACRAMENTO COUNTY

720 9th Street   800 9th Street
Sacramento, CA   Sacramento, CA
(916) 440-6919   (916) 440-5621

All papers are to be filed and hearings held in the Sacramento County Courthouse located at 720 9th Street and Probate documents are filed and hearings held at the Sacramento County Courthouse located at 800 9th Street in Sacramento. The initial hearing date is usually set within four (4) to six (6) weeks. Appointments for mediation are set at that time, usually three (3) weeks away. A pre-mediation orientation is offered. Attorneys can be involved in mediation, but the mediators prefer that they are not. This is determined on a case-by-case basis. Mediation is non-confidential and mediators do make recommendations to the court. In grandparent guardianship cases, the investigation is handled by the Probate Department investigator.

There is very limited on-street parking available within several blocks of the courthouse. Parking lots are within walking distance of two to three blocks and are costly; $.75 to $1.00 per hour. Metal detectors are in use in all courts.

SAN BENITO COUNTY

440 5th Street #206
Hollister, CA
(408) 637-4057

All papers are to be filed and hearings held in the San Benito County Superior Court. The initial hearing date can be obtained in three (3) weeks. Petitioners can pick their own date (check with the clerk) for Law & Motion on Tuesdays at 1:30 p.m. The mediators are in court and the judge orders the parties to make an appointment right then and continues the hearing to await the mediator's report. Attorneys do not participate in the mediation process. Mediation is non-confidential and mediators do make recommendations to the court, if requested by the parties or the court. The court mediator usually conducts the investigation in grandparent guardianship cases.

Parking near the courthouse is free, but scarce. Parking lots are located behind the courthouse and across the street; on-street parking is available within one to two blocks. No metal detectors are in use in the courthouse at this time.

SAN BERNARDINO COUNTY

CENTRAL REGION

351 N. Arrowhead
San Bernardino, CA
(909) 387-6500

17780 Arrow Hwy.
Fontana, CA
(909) 356-6472

216 Brookside Ave.
Redlands, CA
(909) 798-8544

WEST REGION

8303 N. Haven Ave.
Rancho Cucamonga, CA
(909) 945-4131

13260 Central Avenue
Chino, CA
(909) 565-5257

DESERT REGION

14455 Civic Drive
Victorville, CA
(619) 243-8684

235 E. Mt. View St.
Barstow, CA
(619) 256-4817

6527 White Feather Rd.
Joshua Tree, CA
(760) 366-4100

San Bernardino County has eight courts in three regions, Central Region, West Region and Desert Region. Most of the information contained herein applies to San Bernardino (Central) and Rancho Cucamonga (West). Since smaller courts have fewer cases and fewer resources, it is recommended to telephone for further information from the court when ready to file papers. The initial hearing date is set within three (3) to four (4) weeks. In the larger courts, mediation takes place on the date of hearing. A pre-mediation orientation is offered. Attorneys are not involved in the mediation process. Mediation is non-confidential and mediators <u>do make</u> recommendations to the court. In grandparent guardianship cases, the court investigator handles the investigation.

In San Bernardino, free parking is available by the courthouse, usually within one block. No metal detectors are in use at this time. In the smaller courts, parking is available within two blocks.

SAN DIEGO COUNTY

1501-55 Sixth Avenue   220 W. Broadway
San Diego, CA   San Diego, CA
(619) 236-0189   (619) 239-6864

Family Law papers are to be filed and hearings held in the Family Court at 1501 Sixth Avenue in San Diego. Probate papers (guardianships) are to be filed and hearings held in the Probate Division located at 220 West Broadway, San Diego. Upon the filing of papers for grandparent visitation, the clerk sets a hearing date within three (3) to four (4) weeks and a mediation appointment in two (2) to three (3) weeks. If parties are willing to attend mediation in a group of eight (8) to ten (10) people, mediation can be set in five (5) to eight (8) days. Pre-mediation orientation is offered on Thursdays at 5:30 p.m.; doors close at 5:15 p.m. Attorneys are not involved in the mediation process. Mediation is non-confidential and the mediators <u>do make</u> recommendations to the court.

At the Family Court, free street parking is available within several blocks, but there is a two-hour limit which is strictly enforced. There is a parking lot across the street from the courthouse for $5.00 per day. At the Broadway location, there are several parking lots within two blocks of the courthouse and the fee is $10.00 per day. Metal detectors are in use in the both courts.

SAN FRANCISCO COUNTY

400 McAllister Street
San Francisco, CA
(415) 551-3910

All papers are to be filed and hearings held in the Family Law Department for grandparent visitation cases and in the Probate Department for guardianship cases in the San Francisco County Superior Court. It takes three (3) to four (4) weeks to get an initial hearing. If mediation is ordered, it takes place that day. A pre-mediation group orientation is required. Participation of attorneys in mediation in San Francisco has been successful. The mediator sees the attorney(s) first, then the parties, then the attorneys and parties to see if an agreement can be reached. Mediation is confidential and the mediators <u>do not make</u> recommendations to the court. In grandparent guardianship cases, the investigation is handled by either the Probate Department or Family Court Services as assigned by the judge.

There is no on-street parking. Most parking lots are south of Market Street three to four blocks from the courthouse and fees run about $2.00 per hour. Metal detectors are in use in the courts.

SAN JOAQUIN COUNTY

222 E. Weber Avenue #303
Stockton, CA
(209) 468-2355

All papers are to be filed in the San Joaquin County Superior Court and hearings held in the Family Law Department for grandparent visitation cases or in the Probate Department for guardianship cases. It takes about three (3) weeks to get an initial hearing date. Mediation is set on the day of hearing. All parties are allowed to bring an attorney to the mediation hearing. Mediation is non-confidential and the mediators do make recommendations to the court. In grandparent guardianship cases, the court investigator will handle the investigation only if there is a criminal file on the grandparents.

There is little on-street parking. Parking lots are available within three or four blocks; the cost is less than $10.00 per day. Metal detectors are in use in the courthouse.

SAN LUIS OBISPO COUNTY

1035 Palm Street, Room 385
San Luis Obispo, CA
(805) 781-5243

All papers are to be filed in the San Luis Obispo Superior Court and hearings held in the Family Law Department for grandparent visitation cases or in the Probate Department for guardianship cases. It takes three (3) to four (4) weeks to get an initial hearing date. If mediation is not accomplished before the hearing date, the judge orders and continues the hearing. A pre-mediation packet is sent to everyone. It is the responsibility of the petitioner to set a mediation date and this can be done on the day of hearing if the court knows ahead of time. Attorneys are not usually involved in the mediation process. Mediation is confidential and the mediators do not make recommendations to the court. In grandparent guardianship cases, the investigator from the Probate Division handles the investigation.

Parking is available in a parking garage within two blocks of the courthouse. Rates are $.50 per hour and the first hour is free. There are no metal detectors in use in the courthouse at this time.

SAN MATEO COUNTY

401 Marshall Street
Redwood City, CA
(415) 363-4000

All papers are to be filed in the San Mateo County Superior Court and hearings held in the Family Law Department for grandparent visitation cases and in the Probate Department for guardianship case. It takes five (5) to six (6) weeks to get an initial hearing date. If it is an Order to Show case and the judge indicates it is to be set for mediation, the clerk sets the appointment in about four (4) weeks. There is a film on mediation shown in the waiting rooms. In court, the judge can also order mediation for that day as mediators are in court. Attorneys are not usually involved in the mediation process. Mediation is non-confidential and the mediators <u>do make</u> recommendations to the court. In grandparent guardianship cases, Child Protective Services handles the investigation.

There is plenty of free parking in lots within one to two blocks of the courthouse. There are no metal detectors in use in the courthouse at this time.

SANTA BARBARA COUNTY

1100 Anacapa Street
Santa Barbara, CA
(805) 568-2220

All papers are to be filed in the Santa Barbara County Superior Court with hearings held in the Family Law Department for grandparent visitation cases or in the Probate Department for guardianship cases. It takes about three (3) weeks to get an initial hearing date. Mediation often takes place at the courthouse on the date of hearing. If not, the judge will order mediation and the petitioner will make an appointment through the mediator's office. This usually takes two weeks. Attorneys may meet briefly with the mediator prior to the actual mediation meeting. Mediation is confidential and the mediators <u>do not make</u> recommendations to the court. There is no pre-mediation orientation, however, there is an informational class--Children in the Middle--which is required. In grandparent guardianship matters, the investigation is handled by the court investigators through the Probation Department.

There are parking lots within two blocks of the courthouse; 90-minute parking is free, $1.00 per hour thereafter. Metal detectors are in use in the courthouse.

SANTA CLARA COUNTY

170 Park Center Plaza
San Jose, CA
(408) 299-3741

191 N. First Street
San Jose, CA
(408) 299-2964

All papers for Family Law matters are filed and hearings held in the Family Law Division located at 170 Park Center Plaza. All papers for guardianships are filed and hearings held in the Probate Division located at 191 N. First Street. It takes about a month to get an initial hearing. The clerk advises the petitioner to sign up for mediation through Family Court Services. It usually takes four (4) weeks to get a mediation appointment; an emergency assessment can be done on the hearing date. If there is an agreement, the parties can go back on the short-cause calendar; if not, the matter is set for trial. When there is no agreement between the parties, most of the cases are referred to an evaluator. A pre-mediation class is required. Attorneys are not involved in the mediation process. Mediation is confidential and the mediators do not make recommendations to the court. In grandparent guardianship cases, the investigation is handled by the Probate Department court investigator.

Street parking is limited. Parking lots within one block of the courts are $10.00 per day. Parking lots within two to three blocks are $3.00 or $4.00 per day. Metal detectors are in use in all courts.

SANTA CRUZ COUNTY

701 Ocean Street
Santa Cruz, CA
(408) 454-2380

All papers are to be filed and hearings held in the Santa Cruz County Superior Court. It takes thirty (30) days to get an initial hearing date. After mediation is ordered, an appointment can be made by the petitioner within two (2) weeks. A three-hour workshop is required. Attorneys are not involved in the mediation process. Mediation is confidential and mediators do not make recommendations to the court. In grandparent guardianship cases, the investigation is assigned to the Probation Department.

Street parking is limited. There is a free parking lot within one block of the courthouse with a two-hour limit. There is a metal detector available for use in any of the courts.

SHASTA COUNTY

1500 Court Street
Redding, CA
(530) 245-6789

All papers are to be filed in the Shasta County Superior Court and hearings held in the Family Law Department for grandparent visitation or in the Probate Department for guardianship cases. The initial hearing date can be obtained in less than a month by contacting the clerk. The matter will be set on the Law & Motion calendar on Monday. When mediation is ordered, it is assigned by whether or not there is an attorney or the party is in Pro Per, which means representing themselves. A pre-mediation orientation is required. Attorneys are not involved in the mediation process, but may attend the settlement conference. The mediation process is non-confidential and the mediators <u>do make</u> recommendations to the court. In grandparent guardianship cases, the investigation is handled by the mediation office.

On-street metered parking is available around the courthouse, usually within one block. The cost is $.25 for one-half hour. At the present time, entry to the courthouse is restricted and a metal detector will soon be in use.

SIERRA COUNTY

Courthouse Square
Downieville, CA
(916) 289-3698

All papers are to be filed and hearings held in the Sierra County Superior Court. An initial hearing date can be obtained from the clerk in as little as three (3) weeks. When mediation is ordered, the petitioner makes the appointment in the Probation Department. Attorneys are not involved in mediation. Mediation is non-confidential and mediators <u>do make</u> recommendations to the court. In grandparent guardianship matters, the investigation is handled by the Probation Department.

Free parking is available within two blocks of the courthouse either on the street or in a small parking lot. There are no metal detectors in use at this time.

SISKIYOU COUNTY

311 4th Street
Yreka, CA
(530) 842-8082

There is one Superior Court judge in Siskiyou County, but two additional judges may be assigned. All papers are to be filed and held in that court. It can take up to a month to get an initial hearing. When the judge orders mediation, the clerk for the mediator will telephone to set up the appointment. Attorneys do not participate in mediation. Mediation is non-confidential and the mediators do make recommendations to the court, as requested. In grandparent guardianship cases, the investigation is handled by the mediator's office.

There is plenty of free parking lots and on-street parking within one block of the courthouse. There are no metal detectors in use at the present time.

SOLANO COUNTY

600 Union Avenue
Fairfield, CA
(707) 421-7827

There is a Division of Family Law/Probate/Adoptions in the Solano County Superior Court in which papers are to be filed and hearings held. There is no backlog in this court, so getting a hearing date is merely a matter of calling the clerk and picking the date. If the judge orders mediation, the petitioner completes a form and goes to the mediator's desk to set an appointment. This usually takes one week. A pre-mediation orientation is required; there are two speakers on policies and a mediator speaks on the mediation process. The mediators divide the county geographically. Attorneys are not welcome in mediation. The process is confidential and the mediators do not make recommendations to the court unless specifically requested by the judge. In grandparent guardianship cases, the investigation is handled by the court investigator.

Free parking is available in parking lots and on the street within one to two blocks of the courthouse. Metal detectors are in use at the courthouse.

SONOMA COUNTY

600 Administration Drive
Santa Rosa, CA
(707) 527-1100

All papers are to be filed and hearings held in the Superior Court located at 600 Administration Drive. The petitioner should contact the clerk for a hearing date which can be up to eight (8) weeks away. Mediation is to be completed before the hearing and the clerk will set the appointment when papers are filed. Attorneys do not participate in the mediation process. Mediation is non-confidential and mediators do make recommendations to the court.

Free long and short-term parking is available in parking lots within two blocks of the courthouse and ticketed immediately if over the time limit. Metal detectors are in use at the courthouse.

STANISLAUS COUNTY

800 Eleventh Street
Modesto, CA
(209) 558-6000

All papers are to be filed in the Stanislaus County Superior Court and hearings will be held in the Family Law Department or in the Probate Department in a guardianship case. Mediation is conducted the same day as the hearing in the jury room next to the family court department. Contact the clerk for a hearing date, usually set six (6) to eight (8) weeks away. Mediators are available in court on a rotating schedule and cases are assigned to the mediator on duty that day. A pre-mediation orientation is required and is offered each Wednesday at 3:00 p.m. Attorneys participate in mediation. Mediation is non-confidential and mediators do make recommendations to the court. Grandparent guardianship investigations are handled by the court investigator's office. If mediation is ordered in a guardianship case, the same procedure is followed.

On-street parking is limited and closely monitored. There is a parking garage located on Eleventh Street between I and J Streets (less than two blocks from the courthouse); fees are $.50 per hour. There is a metal detector in use at the courthouse.

SUTTER COUNTY

446 Second Street
Yuba City, CA
(916) 822-7360

All papers are to be filed and hearings held in the Sutter County Superior Court. The initial hearing date can be obtained by contacting the clerk and having the matter set on the Law & Motion calendar on Mondays at 9:00 a.m. If the judge orders mediation, the mediator is in court and an appointment can be made at that time, usually within two weeks. Mediation is possible on the same date if the parties are from out of town. Attorneys do not participate in mediation. The mediation process is confidential and the mediators <u>may or may not make</u> recommendations to the court, depending on the circumstances of the case.

Free parking is available in lots and on the street within two or three blocks of the courthouse. There are no metal detectors in use at this time in civil courts, but all persons entering the courthouse are subject to search.

TEHAMA COUNTY

633 Washington Street
Red Bluff, CA
(916) 527-6441

All papers are to be filed and hearings held in the Tehama County Superior Court. An initial hearing date can be obtained by clearing it with the clerk, usually within three weeks. The matter is set on the Law & Motion calendar on Mondays at 1:45 p.m. If mediation is ordered, the appointment can be set in court with the mediator. Parties are given a form and booklet to prepare for the mediation appointment which is set within a week. Attorneys do not participate in the mediation process. Mediation is non-confidential and mediators <u>do make</u> recommendations to the court. Grandparent guardianship cases are assigned to the Chief Executive's Office by the judge.

Free parking is available on the street within two blocks. There are some pay lots within two blocks; the cost is $.10 per one-half hour. There are no metal detectors in use at this time.

TRINITY COUNTY

101 Court Street
Weaverville, CA
(530) 623-1208

There is one Superior Court in Trinity County and all papers are to be filed and hearings held at the Trinity County Courthouse. Mediation usually takes place at the time of hearing; if an appointment is needed, it is usually within two (2) weeks. Parties are encouraged, however, to see the mediator prior to the hearing. A hearing date can be obtained from the clerk and the matter is placed on the Law & Motion calendar on the second and fourth Mondays. Printed information and forms are available regarding mediation. Attorneys do not participate in the mediation process. Mediation is non-confidential and mediators <u>do make</u> recommendations to the judge. In grandparent guardianship cases, the investigation is handled by the probate investigator.

Free street parking is available around the courthouse within one block. There are no metal detectors in use at this time.

TULARE COUNTY

Civic Center
Visalia, CA
(209) 733-6374

All papers are to be filed and hearings held in the Tulare County Superior Court. Mediation is usually handled the same day as the hearing. A short orientation is required. To obtain an initial hearing date, parties with counsel contact the calendar clerk; parties without counsel contact the regular court clerk. It takes four (4) to five (5) weeks to get a hearing date. Attorneys do not participate in mediation. Mediation is non-confidential and the mediators <u>do make</u> recommendations to the court. In grandparent guardianship cases, the investigation is handled by Family Court Services. The judge can request an investigation by Child Protective Services.

There is a free parking lot within one block of the courthouse with a two-hour limit; tickets are issued regularly if the limit is exceeded. Free all day parking is available two blocks from the courthouse. Very little street parking is available. Metal detectors are not in use at this time.

TUOLUMNE COUNTY

41 W. Yaney Avenue
Sonora, CA
(209) 533-5675

All papers are to be filed and hearings held in the Tuolumne County Superior Court. Mediation can take place on the date of hearing or if an appointment is necessary, the mediation secretary will schedule in about two (2) weeks. Attorneys are not involved in the mediation process. Mediation is confidential and the mediators <u>do not</u> make recommendations to the court. In grandparent guardianship cases, the judge will appoint a local attorney to do the investigation.

Free two-hour parking is available on the street and in the parking garage across the street from the courthouse. A side street is available within two or three blocks. Metal detectors are in use in the courthouse.

VENTURA COUNTY

800 S. Victoria Avenue
Ventura, CA
(805) 662-6620

All papers are to be filed in the Ventura County Superior Court and hearings will be held in either the Family Law or Probate Divisions. It takes four (4) to six (6) weeks to get an initial hearing date. If parties anticipate mediation, it would be best to get the mediation complete before the hearing to save time. Appointments can be made through Family Court Services. A pre-mediation orientation is required and is offered every Thursday evening; the orientation is offered in Spanish one Thursday per month. Attorneys do not participate in the mediation process. Mediation is non-confidential and mediators <u>do make</u> recommendations to the court. In grandparent guardianship cases, the investigation is handled by the court investigator.

Free parking lots are available within three blocks of the courthouse; on-street parking is somewhat limited. Both metal detectors and security guards are used in the courthouse.

YOLO COUNTY

725 Court Street
Woodland, CA
(916) 666-8598

All papers are to be filed and hearings held in the Yolo County Superior Court. Mediation takes place the same day as the hearing. To obtain a hearing date, contact the clerk. You can pick your own date from the Law & Motion calendar which is held every day at 9:00 a.m. Be sure and allow time for process of service. The only participation of attorneys in mediation is to prepare orders after an agreement is reached. Mediation is non-confidential and the mediators <u>do make</u> recommendations to the court. In grandparent guardianship cases, the investigation is handled by a local attorney appointed by the judge.

Free on-street parking and parking lots are available within two blocks of the courthouse. Metal detectors are not in use at this time.

YUBA COUNTY

215 Fifth Street
Marysville, CA
(916) 741-6258

All papers are to be filed and hearings held in the Yuba County Superior Court, on the Law & Motion Calendar which is set on Mondays at 11:00 a.m.. Mediation is to take place one (1) week prior to the hearing. After getting a hearing date from the clerk, usually three (3) weeks away, a brief orientation video is offered at that time. Attorneys do not participate in mediation. Mediation is confidential and the mediators <u>do not make</u> recommendations to the court. In grandparent guardianship cases, the investigation is handled by the court investigator.

Free parking is available on the street within one to two blocks with a two-hour time limit. The time limit is monitored closely. Free parking lots are located within two blocks. Hand-held metal detectors are available for use as needed.

DISCLAIMER BY AUTHOR

The information on the chart was taken from <u>Profile Child Custody Mediation & Evaluation Services in California Superior Courts</u>. The individual county information was obtained by telephoning each county clerk's office in each county. An attempt was made to speak to the person most knowledgeable about grandparent visitation and grandparent guardianship cases. The courts always have the option of changing their processes and it is common to find changes. There is also an exception related to how soon a court date can be obtained. In emergency restraining order situations, the court date may be no more than twenty days from the date the papers are filed. Guardianships are always set at least forty-five days from the date of filing in order for the investigator's report to be completed.

PERSONAL NOTES:

California Family Code

PART 1 - CUSTODY OF CHILDREN

CHAPTER 1 - DEFINITIONS

Section 3000   Scope of Definitions

Unless the Provision or context otherwise requires, the definitions in this chapter govern the construction of this Division.

Section 3002   Joint Custody

"Joint Custody" means joint physical custody and joint legal custody.

Section 3003   Joint Legal Custody

"Joint legal custody" means that both parents shall share the right and the responsibility to make the decisions relating to the health, education, and welfare of a child.

Section 3004   Joint Physical Custody

"Joint physical custody" means that each of the parents shall have significant periods of physical custody. Joint physical custody shall be shared by the parents in such a way so as to assure a child of frequent and continuing contact with both parents, subject to Sections 3011 and 3020.

Section 3006   Sole Legal Custody

"Sole legal custody" means that one parent shall have the right and the responsibility to make the decisions relating to the health, education, and welfare of a child.

Section 3007   Sole Physical Custody

"Sole physical custody" means that a child shall reside with and be under the supervision of one parent, subject to the power of the court to order visitation.

CHAPTER 2 - GENERAL PROVISIONS

Section 3010   Right to Custody, Services and Earnings of Unemancipated Minor

(a) The mother of an unemancipated minor child and the father, if presumed to be the father under Section 7611, are equally entitled to the custody of the child.

(b) If one parent is dead, is unable or refuses to take custody, or has abandoned the child, the other parent is entitled to custody of the child.

Section 3011   Factors Determining Best Interest of Child

In making a determination of the best interest of the child in a proceeding described in Section 3021, the court shall, among any other factors it finds relevant, consider all of the following:

(a) The health, safety, and welfare of the child.

(b) Any history of abuse by one parent or any other person seeking custody against any of the following:

(1) Any child to whom he or she is related by blood or affinity or with whom he or she has had a caretaking relationship, no matter how temporary.

(2) The other parent.

(3) A parent, current spouse, or cohabitant, of the parent or person seeking custody, or a person with whom the parent or person seeking custody has a dating or engagement relationship. As a prerequisite to the consideration of allegations of abuse, the court may require substantial independent corroboration, including, but not limited to, written reports by law enforcement agencies, child protective services or other social welfare agencies, courts, medical facilities, or other public agencies or private nonprofit organizations providing services to victims of sexual assault or domestic violence. As used in this subdivision, "abuse against a child," means "child abuse" as defined in Section 11165.6 of the Penal Code and abuse against any of the other persons described in paragraph (2) or (3) means "abuse" as defined in Section 6203 of this code.

(c) The nature and amount of contact with both parents.

(d) The habitual or continual illegal use of controlled substances or habitual or continual abuse of alcohol by either parent. Before considering these allegations, the court may first require independent corroboration, including, but not limited to, written reports from law enforcement agencies, courts, probation departments, social welfare agencies, medical facilities, rehabilitation facilities, or other public agencies or nonprofit organizations providing drug and alcohol abuse services. As used in this subdivision, "controlled substances" has the same meaning as defined in the California Uniform Controlled Substances Act, Division 10 (commencing with Section 11000) of the Health and Safety Code.

(e)(1) Where allegations about a parent pursuant to subdivision (b) or (d) have been brought to the attention of the court in the current proceeding, and the court makes an order for sole or joint custody to that parent, the court shall state its reasons in writing or on the record. In these circumstances, the court shall ensure that any order regarding custody or visitation is specific as to time, day, place, and manner of transfer of the child as set forth in subdivision (b) of Section 6323.

(2) The provisions of this subdivision shall not apply if the parties stipulate in writing or on the record regarding custody or visitation.

PART 2 - RIGHT TO CUSTODY OF MINOR CHILD

CHAPTER 1 - GENERAL PROVISIONS

Section 3020   Legislative Findings and Declaration

(a) The Legislature finds and declares that it is the public policy of this state to assure that the health, safety, and welfare of children shall be the court's primary concern in determining the best interests of children when making any orders regarding the custody or visitation of children. The Legislature further finds and declares that the perpetration of child abuse or domestic violence in a household where a child resides is detrimental to the child.

(b) The Legislature finds and declares that it is the public policy of this state to assure that children have frequent and continuing contact with both parents after the parents have separated or dissolved their marriage, or ended their relationship, and to encourage parents to share the rights and responsibilities of child rearing in order to effect this policy, except where the contact would not be in the best interest of the child, as provided in Section 3011.

(c) Where the policies set forth in subdivisions (a) and (b) of this section are in conflict, any court's order regarding custody or visitation shall be made in a manner that ensures the health, safety, and welfare of the child and the safety of all family members.

Section 3021   Application

This part applies in any of the following:

(a) A proceeding for dissolution of marriage.

(b) A proceeding for nullity of marriage.

(c) A proceeding for legal separation of the parties.

(d) An action for exclusive custody pursuant to Section 3120.

(e) A proceeding to determine custody or visitation in a proceeding pursuant to the Domestic Violence Prevention Act (Division 10 (commencing with Section 6200). In an action under Section 6323, nothing in this subdivision shall be construed to authorize custody or visitation rights to be granted to any party to a Domestic Violence Prevention Act proceeding who has not established a parent and child relationship pursuant to paragraph (2) of subdivision (a) of Section 6323.

(f) A proceeding to determine custody or visitation in an action pursuant to the Uniform Parentage Act (Part 3 (commencing with Section 7600) of Division 12).

(g) A proceeding to determine custody or visitation in an action brought by the District Attorney pursuant to Section 11350.1 of the Welfare and Institutions Code.

Section 3022   Courts' Power to Determine Custody

The court may, during the pendency of a proceeding or at any time thereafter, make an order for the custody of a child during minority that seems necessary or proper.

Section 3022.5   Effect of Conviction in Connection with False Accusation on Reconsideration Motion

A motion by a parent for reconsideration of an existing child custody order shall be granted if the motion is based on the fact that the other parent was convicted of a crime in connection with falsely accusing the moving parent of child abuse.

Section 3023   Contested Issues of Custody Gets Priority

(a) If custody of a minor child is the sole contested issue, the case shall be given preference over other civil cases, except matters to which special precedence may be given by law, for assigning a trial date and shall be given an early hearing.

(b) If there is more than one contested issue and one of the issues is the custody of a minor child, the court, as to the issue of custody, shall order a separate trial. The separate trial shall be given preference over other civil cases, except matters to which special precedence may be given by law, for assigning a trial date.

Section 3024   Notice of Change of Child's Residence

In making an order for custody, if the court does not consider it inappropriate, the court may specify that a parent shall notify the other parent if the parent plans to change the residence of the child for more than 30 days, unless there is prior written agreement to the removal. The notice shall be given before the contemplated move, by mail, return receipt requested, postage prepaid, to the last known address of the parent to be notified. A copy of the notice shall also be sent to that parent's counsel of record. To the extent feasible, the notice shall be provided within a minimum of 45 days before the proposed change of residence so as to allow time for mediation of a new agreement concerning custody. This section does not affect orders made before January 1, 1989.

Section 3025   Access to Child's Records by Noncustodial Parent

Notwithstanding any other provision of law, access to records and information pertaining to a minor child, including, but not limited to medical, dental, and school records, shall not be denied to a parent because that parent is not the child's custodial parent.

Section 3026   Family Reunification Services Not to Be Ordered

Family reunification services shall not be ordered as a part of a child custody or visitation rights proceeding. Nothing in this section affects the applicability of Section 16507 of the Welfare and Institutions Code.

Section 3027   False Accusation of Child Abuse or Neglect-Sanctions

(a) If a court determines that an accusation of child abuse or neglect made during a child custody proceeding is false and the person making the accusation knew it to be false at the time the accusation was made, the court may impose reasonable money sanctions, not to exceed all costs incurred by the party accused as a direct result of defending the accusation, and reasonable attorneys' fees incurred in recovering the sanctions, against the person making the accusation. For the purpose of this section, "person" includes a witness, a party, or a party's attorney.

(b) On motion by any person requesting sanctions under this section, the court shall issue its order to show cause why the requested sanctions should not be imposed. The order to show cause shall be served on the person against whom the sanctions are sought and a hearing thereon shall be scheduled by the court to be conducted at least 15 days after the order is served.

(c) The remedy provided by this section is in addition to any other remedy provided by law.

Section 3028   Amount of Compensation for Failing to Assume Caretaker Role or for Obstructing Visitation Rights

(a) The court may order financial compensation for periods when a parent fails to assume the caretaker responsibility or when a parent has been thwarted by the other parent when attempting to exercise custody or visitation rights contemplated by a custody or visitation order, including, but not limited to, an order for joint physical custody, or by a written or oral agreement between the parents.

(b) The compensation shall be limited to (1) the reasonable expenses incurred for or on behalf of a child, resulting from the other parent's failure to assume caretaker responsibility or (2) the reasonable expenses incurred by a parent for or on behalf of a child resulting from the other parent's thwarting of the parent's efforts to exercise custody or visitation rights. The expenses may include the value of a caretaker services but are not limited to the cost of services provided by a third party during the relevant period.

(c) The compensation may be requested by noticed motion or an order to show cause which shall allege, under penalty of perjury (1) a minimum of one hundred dollars ($100) of expenses incurred or (2) at least three occurrences of failure to exercise custody or visitation rights or (3) at least three occurrences of the thwarting of efforts to exercise custody or visitation rights within the six months before filing of the motion or order.

(d) Attorney's fees shall be awarded to the prevailing party upon a showing of the non-prevailing party's ability to pay as required by Section 270.

Section 3029   Amount of Compensation From Noncustodial Parent in Addition to Public Assistance

An order granting custody to a parent who is receiving or in the opinion of the court is likely to receive, assistance pursuant to the Family Economic Security Act of 1982 (Chapter 2 commencing with Section 11200 of Part 3 of Division 9 of the Welfare and Institutions Code) for the maintenance of the child shall include an order pursuant to Chapter 2 (commencing with Section 4000) of Part 2 of Division 9 of this code, directing the non- custodial parent to pay any amount necessary for the support of the child, to the extent of the noncustodial parent's ability to pay.

Section 3030   Conviction under Penal Code or Registration as Sex Offender as Grounds for Denial of Custody or Visitation

(a) No person shall be granted custody of, or unsupervised visitation with, a child if the person is required to be registered as a sex offender of Section 290 of the Penal Code where the victim was a minor, or if the person has been convicted under Section 273a, 273d, 647.6 of the Penal Code, unless the court finds that there is no significant risk to the child.

(b) No person shall be granted custody of, or visitation with, a child if the person has been convicted under Section 261 of the Penal Code and the child was conceived as a result of that violation.

(c) The court may order child support that is to be paid by a person subject to subdivision (a) or (b) to be paid through the district attorney's office, as authorized by Section 4573 of the Family Code and Section 11475.1 of the Welfare and Institutions Code.

(d) The court shall not disclose, or cause to be disclosed, the custodial parent's place of residence, place of employment, or the child's school, unless the court finds that the disclosure would be in the best interests of the child.

Section 3031   Restraining or Protective Orders as Grounds for Denial of Custody

(a) Where the court considers the issue of custody or visitation the court is encouraged to make a reasonable effort to ascertain whether or not any emergency protective order, protective order, or other restraining order is in effect that concerns the parties or the minor. The court is encouraged not to make a custody or visitation order that is inconsistent with the emergency protective order, protective order, or other restraining order, unless the court makes both of the following findings:

(1) The custody or visitation order cannot be made consistent with the emergency protective order, protective order, or other restraining order.

(2) The custody or visitation order is in the best interest of the minor.

(b) Whenever custody or visitation is granted to a parent in a case in which domestic violence is alleged and an emergency protective order, protective order, or other restraining order has been issued, the custody or visitation order shall specify the time, day, place, and manner of transfer of the child for custody or visitation to limit the child's exposure to potential domestic conflict or violence and to ensure the safety of all family members. Where the court finds a party is staying in a place designated as a shelter for victims of domestic violence or other confidential location, the court's order for time, day, place, and manner of transfer of the child for custody or visitation shall be designed to prevent disclosure of the location of the shelter or other confidential location.

(c) When making an order for custody or visitation in a case in which domestic violence is alleged and an emergency protective order, protective order, or other restraining order has been issued, the court shall consider whether the best interest of the child, based upon the circumstances of the case, requires that any custody or visitation arrangement shall be limited to situations in which a third person, specified by the court, is present, or whether custody or visitation shall be suspended or denied.

CHAPTER 2 -MATTERS TO BE CONSIDERED IN GRANTING CUSTODY

Section 3040   Custody Awards; Order of Preference

(a) Custody should be granted in the following order of preference according to the best interest of the child as provided in Section 3011 and 3020.

(1) To both parents jointly pursuant to Chapter 4 (commencing with Section 3080) or to either parent. In making an order granting custody to either parent, the court shall consider, among other factors, which parent is more likely to allow the child frequent and continuing contact with the noncustodial parent, consistent with Section 3011 and 3020, and shall not prefer a parent as custodian because of that parent's sex. The court, in its discretion, may require the parents to submit to the court a plan for the implementation of the custody order.

(2) If to neither parent, to the person or persons in whose home the child has been living in a wholesome and stable environment.

(3) To any other person or persons deemed by the court to be suitable and able to provide adequate and proper care and guidance for the child.

(b) This section establishes neither a preference nor a presumption for or against joint legal custody, joint physical custody, or sole custody, but allows the court and the family the widest discretion to choose a parenting plan that is in the best interest of the child.

Section 3041   Finding Necessary for Nonparental Custody Award

Before making an order granting custody to a person or persons other than a parent, without the consent of the parents, the court shall make a finding that granting custody to a parent would be detrimental to the child and that granting custody to the nonparent is required to serve the best interest of the child. Allegations that parental custody would be detrimental to the child, other than a statement of that ultimate fact, shall not appear in the pleading. The court may, in its discretion, exclude the public from the hearing on this issue.

Section 3042   Consideration of Child's Preference

(a) If a child is of sufficient age and capacity to reason so as to form an intelligent preference as to custody, the court shall consider and give due weight to the wishes of the child in making an order granting or modifying custody.

(b) In addition to the requirements of subdivision (b) of Section 765 of the Evidence Code, the court shall control the examination of the child witness so as to protect the best interests of the child. The court may preclude the calling of the child as a witness where the best interests of the child so dictate and may provide alternative means of obtaining information regarding the child's preferences.

Section 3043   Nomination of Guardian

In determining the person or persons to whom custody should be granted under paragraph (2) or (3) of subdivision (a) of Section 3040, the court shall consider and give due weight to the nomination of a guardian of the person of the child by a parent under Article 1 (commencing with Section 1500) of Chapter 1 of Part 2 of Division 4 of the Probate Code.

CHAPTER 3-TEMPORARY CUSTODY ORDER DURING PENDENCY OF PROCEEDING

Section 3060   Petition for Temporary Restraining Order

A petition for a temporary custody order, containing the statement required by Section 3409, may be included with the initial filing of the petition or action or may be filed at any time after the initial filing.

Section 3061   Parental Agreement or Understanding on Custody

If the parties have agreed to or reached an understanding on the custody or temporary custody of their children, a copy of the agreement or an affidavit as to their understanding shall be attached to the petition or action. As promptly as possible after this filing, the court shall, except in exceptional circumstances, enter an order granting temporary custody in accordance with the agreement or understanding or in accordance with any stipulation of the parties.

Section 3062   Ex Parte Temporary Custody Order and Order to Show Cause

(a) In the absence of an agreement, understanding, or stipulation, the court may, if jurisdiction is appropriate, enter an ex parte temporary custody order, set a hearing date within 20 days, and issue an order to show cause on the responding party.   If the responding party does not appear or respond within the time set, the temporary custody order may be extended as necessary, pending the termination of the proceedings.

(b) If, despite good faith efforts, service of the ex parte order and order to show cause has not been effected in a timely fashion and there is reason to believe, based on an affidavit, or other manner of proof made under penalty of perjury, by the petitioner, that the responding party has possession of the minor child and seeks to avoid the jurisdiction of the court or is concealing the whereabouts of the child, then the hearing date may be reset and the ex parte order extended up to an additional 90 days. After service has been effected, either party may request ex parte that the hearing date be advanced or the ex parte order be dissolved or modified.

Section 3063   Restraint on Removal of Child from State

In conjunction with any ex parte order seeking or modifying an order of custody, the court shall enter an order restraining the person receiving custody from removing the child from the state pending notice and a hearing on the order seeking or modifying custody.

Section 3064   Ex Parte Order Modifying or Granting Custody Order-Risk of Removal or Immediate Harm to Child

The court shall refrain from making an order granting or modifying a custody order on an ex parte basis unless there has been a showing of immediate harm to the child or immediate risk that the child will be removed from the State of California.   "Immediate harm to the child" includes having a parent who has committed acts of domestic violence, where the court determines that the acts of domestic violence are of recent origin or are a part of a demonstrated and continuing pattern of acts of domestic violence.

CHAPTER 4 - JOINT CUSTODY

Section 3080   Joint Custody Presumption

There is a presumption, affecting the burden of proof, that joint custody is in the best interest of a minor child, subject to Section 3011, where the parents have agreed to joint custody or so agree in open court at a hearing for the purpose of determining the custody of the minor child.

Section 3081   Application by Parents and Court Investigation

On application of either parent, joint custody may be ordered in the discretion of the court in cases other than those described in Section 3080, subject to Section 3011.   For the purpose of assisting the court in making a determination whether joint custody is appropriate under this section, the court may direct that an investigation be conducted pursuant to Chapter 6 (commencing with Section 3110).

Section 3082   Statement of Court's Reason in Granting or Denying Request

When a request for joint custody is granted or denied, the court, upon the request of any party, shall state in its decision the reasons for granting or denying the request.   A statement that joint physical custody is, or is not, in the best interest of the child is not sufficient to satisfy the requirements of this section.

Section 3083   Guidelines for Joint Custody Order

In making an order of joint legal custody, the court shall specify the circumstances under which the consent of both parents is required to be obtained in order to exercise legal control of the child and the consequences of the failure to obtain mutual consent.   In all other circumstances, either parent acting alone may exercise legal control of the child.   An order of joint legal custody shall not be construed to permit an action that is inconsistent with the physical custody order unless the action is expressly authorized by the court.

Section 3084   Enumeration of Rights of Parent to Physical Control Child

In making an order of joint physical custody, the court shall specify the rights of each parent to physical control of the child in sufficient detail to enable a parent deprived of that control to implement laws for relief of child snatching and kidnapping.

Section 3085   Joint Legal Custody Absent Joint Physical Custody

In making an order for custody with respect to both parents, the court may grant joint legal custody without granting joint physical custody.

Section 3086   Designations of Primary Caretaker and Primary Home for Joint Legal or Physical Custody

In making an order of joint physical custody or joint legal custody, the court may specify one parent as the primary caretaker of the child and one home as the primary home of the child, for the purposes of determining eligibility for public assistance.

Section 3087   Modification or Termination of Joint Custody Order

An order for joint custody may be modified or terminated upon the petition of one or both parents or on the court's own motion if it is shown that the best interest of the child requires modification or termination of the order. If either parent opposes the modification or termination order, the court shall state in its decision the reasons for modification or termination of the joint custody order.

Section 3088   Modification of Custody Order to Joint Custody Order

An order for the custody of a minor child entered by a court in this state or any other state may, subject to the jurisdictional requirements in Sections 3403 and 3414, be modified at any time to an order for joint custody in accordance with this chapter.

Section 3089   Consultation With Family Conciliation Court

In counties having a conciliation court, the court or the parties may, at any time, pursuant to local rules of court, consult with the conciliation court for the purpose of assisting the parties to formulate a plan for implementation of the custody order or to resolve a controversy which has arisen in the implementation of a plan for custody.

CHAPTER 5 - VISITATION RIGHTS

Section 3100   Grounds for Granting Visitation-Domestic Violence Prevention Order a Factor

(a) In making an order pursuant to Chapter 4 (commencing with section 3080), the court shall grant reasonable visitation rights to a parent unless it is shown that the visitation would be detrimental to the best interest of the child. In the discretion of the court, reasonable visitation rights may be granted to any other person having an interest in the welfare of the child.

(b) If a protective order, as defined in Section 6218, has been directed to a parent, the court shall consider whether the best interest of the child requires that any visitation by that parent shall be limited to situations in which a third person, specified by the court, is present, or whether visitation shall be suspended or denied. The court shall include in its deliberations a consideration of the nature of the acts from which the parent was enjoined and the period of time that has elapsed since that order. A parent may submit to the court the name of a person that the parent deems suitable to be present during visitation.

(c) Whenever visitation is ordered in a case in which domestic violence is alleged and an emergency protective order, protective order, or other restraining order has been issued, the visitation order shall specify the time, day, place, and manner of transfer of the child, so as to limit the child's exposure to potential domestic conflict or violence and to ensure the safety of all family members.

(d) Where the court finds a party is staying in a place designated as a shelter for victims of domestic violence or other confidential location, the court's order for time, day, place, and manner of transfer of the child for visitation shall be designed to prevent disclosure of the location of the shelter or other confidential location.

Section 3101   Stepparents Eligible for Visitation Rights

(a) Notwithstanding any other provision of law, the court may grant reasonable visitation to a stepparent, if visitation by the stepparent is determined to be in the best interest of the minor child.

(b) If a protective order, as defined in Section

6218, has been directed to a stepparent to whom visitation may be granted pursuant to this section, the court shall consider whether the best interest of the child requires that any visitation by the stepparent be denied.

(c) Visitation rights may not be ordered under this section that would conflict with a right of custody or visitation of a birth parent who is not a party to the proceeding.

(d) As used in this section:

(1) "Birth parent" means "birth parent" as defined in Section 8512.

(2) "Stepparent" means a person who is a party to the marriage that is the subject of the proceeding, with respect to a minor child of the other party to the marriage.

Section 3102   Visitation Rights When Parents Deceased

(a) If either parent of an unemancipated minor child is deceased, the children, siblings, parents, and grandparents of the deceased parent may be granted reasonable visitation with the child during the child's minority upon a finding that the visitation would be in the best interest of the minor child.

(b) In granting visitation pursuant to this section to a person other than a grandparent of the child, the court shall consider the amount of personal contact between the person and the child before the application for the visitation order.

(c) This section does not apply if the child has been adopted by a person other than a stepparent or grandparent of the child. Any visitation rights granted pursuant to this section before the adoption of the child automatically terminate if the child is adopted by a person other than a stepparent or grandparent of the child.

Section 3103   Grandparents Eligible for Visitation Rights

(a) Notwithstanding any other provision of law, in a proceeding described in Section 3021, the court may grant reasonable visitation to a grandparent of a minor child of a party to the proceeding if the court determines that visitation by the grandparent is in the best interest of the child.

(b) If a protective order as defined in Section 6218 has been directed to the grandparent

during the pendency of the proceeding, the court shall consider whether the best interest of the child requires that visitation by the grandparent be denied.

(c) The petitioner shall give notice of the petition to each of the parents of the child, any stepparent, and any person who has physical custody of the child, by certified mail, return receipt requested, postage prepaid, to the person's last known address, or to the attorneys of record of the parties to the proceeding.

(d) There is a rebuttable presumption affecting the burden of proof that the visitation of a grandparent is not in the best interest of a minor child if the child's parents agree that the grandparent should not be granted visitation rights.

(e) Visitation rights may not be ordered under this section if that would conflict with a right of custody or visitation of a birth parent who is not a party to the proceeding.

(f) Visitation ordered pursuant to this section shall not create a basis for or against a change of residence of the child, but shall be one of the factors for the court to consider in ordering a change of residence.

(g) When a court orders grandparental visitation pursuant to this section, the court in its discretion may, based upon the relevant circumstances of the case:

(1) Allocate the percentage of grandparental visitation between the parents for purposes of the calculation of child support pursuant to the statewide uniform guideline (Article 2 (commencing with Section 4050) of Chapter 2 of Part 2 of Division 9).

(2) Notwithstanding Sections 3930 and 3951, order a parent or grandparent to pay to the other, an amount for the support of the child or grandchild. For purposes of this paragraph, "support" means costs related to visitation such as any of the following:

(A) Transportation.

(B) Provision of basic expenses for the child or grandchild, such as medical expenses, daycare costs, and other necessities.

(h) As used in this section, "birth parent" means "birth parent" as defined in Section 8512.

Section 3104   Grandparent Visitation Rights

(a) On petition to the court by a grandparent of a minor child, the court may grant reasonable visitation rights to the grandparent if the court does both of the following:

(1) Finds that there is a preexisting relationship between the grandparent and the grandchild that has engendered a bond such that visitation is in the best interest of the child.

(2) Balances the interest of the child in having visitation with the grandparent against the right of the parents to exercise their parental authority.

(b) A petition for visitation under this section may not be filed while the natural or adoptive parents are married, unless one or more of the following circumstances exist:

(1) The parents are currently living separately and apart on a permanent or indefinite basis.

(2) One of the parents has been absent for more than one month without the other spouse knowing the whereabouts of the absent spouse.

(3) One of the parents joins in the petition with the grandparents.

(4) The child is not residing with either parent.

At any time that a change of circumstances occurs such that none of these circumstances exist, the parent or parents may move the court to terminate grandparental visitation and the court shall grant the termination.

(c) The petitioner shall give notice of the petition to each of the parents of the child, any stepparent, and any person who has physical custody of the child, by personal service pursuant to Section 415.10 of the Code of Civil Procedure.

(d) If a protective order as defined in Section 6218 has been directed to the grandparent during the pendency of the proceeding, the court shall consider whether the best interest of the child requires that any visitation by that grandparent should be denied.

(e) There is a rebuttable presumption that the visitation of a grandparent is not in the best interest of a minor child if the natural or adoptive parents agree that the grandparent should not be granted visitation rights.

(f) There is a rebuttable presumption affecting the burden of proof that the visitation of a grandparent is not in the best interest of a minor child if the parent who has been awarded sole legal and physical custody of the child in another proceeding or with whom the child resides if there is currently no operative custody order objects to visitation by the grandparent.

(g) Visitation rights may not be ordered under this section if that would conflict with a right of custody or visitation of a birth parent who is not a party to the proceeding.

(h) Visitation ordered pursuant to this section shall not create a basis for or against a change of residence of the child, but shall be one of the factors for the court to consider in ordering change of residence.

(i) When a court orders grandparental visitation pursuant to this section, the court in its discretion may, based upon the relevant circumstances of the case:

(1) Allocate the percentage of grandparental visitation between the parents for purposes of the calculation of child support pursuant to the statewide uniform guideline (Article 2 (commencing with Section 4050) of Chapter 2 of Part 2 of Division 9).

(2) Notwithstanding Section 3930 and 3951, order a parent or grandparent to pay to the other, an amount for the support of the child or grandchild. For purposes of this paragraph, "support" means costs related to visitation such as any of the following:

(A) Transportation.

(B) Provision of basic expenses for the child or grandchild, such as medical expenses, daycare costs, and other necessities.

(j) As used in this section, "birth parent" means "birth parent" as defined in Section 8512.

CHAPTER 6 - CUSTODY INVESTIGATION AND REPORT

Section 3110   Court-Appointed Investigator Defined

As used in this chapter, "court-appointed investigator" means a probation officer, domestic relations investigator, or court-appointed evaluator directed by the court to conduct an investigation pursuant to this chapter.

Section 3111   Court -Ordered Investigation and Report; Filing; Evidentiary Status; Training for Investigators

(a) Where directed by the court, the court-appointed investigator shall conduct a custody investigation and file a written confidential report on it. At least 10 days before any hearing regarding custody of the child, the report shall be filed with the clerk of the court in which the custody hearing will be conducted and served on the parties or their attorneys. The report may be considered by the court.

(b) The report shall not be made available other than as provided in subdivision (a).

(c) The report may be received in evidence on stipulation of all interested parties and is competent evidence as to all matters contained in the report.

(d) On and after January 1, 1998, no person shall be a court-appointed investigator under this chapter unless the person has completed the domestic violence training program described in Section 1816. The Judicial Council shall prescribe standards that the training shall meet.

(e) The Judicial Council shall draft a statewide rule of court requiring domestic violence training for all court-appointed persons who evaluate or investigate child custody matters.

Section 3112   Court Ordered Investigation and Report-Payment for Incurred Expense

(a) Where a court-appointed investigator is directed by the court to conduct a custody investigation or to undertake visitation work, including necessary evaluation, supervision, and reporting, the court shall inquire into the financial condition of the parent, guardian, or the other person charged with the support of the minor. If the court finds the parent, guardian, or other person able to pay all or part of the expense of the investigation, report, and recommendation, the court may make an order requiring the parent, guardian, or the other person to repay the county the amount the court determines proper.

(b) The repayment shall be made to the county officer designated by the board of supervisors, who shall keep suitable accounts of the expenses and repayments and shall deposit the collections in the county treasury.

Section 3113   Conditions for Separate Meetings with Court-Appointed Investigator

Where there has been a history of domestic violence between the parties or where a protective order as defined in Section 6218 is in effect, at the request of the party alleging domestic violence in a written declaration under penalty of perjury or at the request of a party

who is protected by the order, the parties shall meet with the court-appointed investigator separately and at separate times.

Section 3114   Recommendation for Court-Appointed Investigator

Nothing in this chapter prohibits a court-appointed investigator from recommending to the court that counsel be appointed pursuant to Chapter 10 (commencing with Section 3150) to represent the minor child. In making that recommendation, the court-appointed investigator shall inform the court of the reasons why it would be in the best interest of the child to have counsel appointed.

Section 3115   Right to Cross-Examine Court-Appointed Investigation

No statement, whether written or oral, or conduct shall be held to constitute a waiver by party of the right to cross-examine the court-appointed investigator, unless the statement is made, or the conduct occurs, after the report has been received by a party or his or her attorney.

Section 3116   Limitations of Court-Appointed Investigator

Nothing in this chapter limits the duty of a court-appointed investigator to assist the appointing court in the transaction of the business of the court.

Section 3117   Adoption of Standards and Guidelines

The Judicial Council shall, by January 1, 1999, do both of the following:

(a) Adopt standards for full and partial court-connected evaluations, investigations, and assessments related to child custody.

(b) Adopt procedural guidelines for the expeditious and cost-effective cross-examination of court-appointed investigators, including, but not limited to, the use of electronic technology whereby the court-appointed investigator may not need to be present in the courtroom. These guidelines shall in no way limit the requirement that the court-appointed investigator be available for the purposes of cross-examination. These guidelines shall also provide for written notification to the parties of the right to cross-examine these investigators after the parties have had a reasonable time to review the investigators' report.

CHAPTER 7 - ACTION FOR EXCLUSIVE CUSTODY

Section 3120   Child Custody Action Without Petition for Dissolution or Separation
Without filing a petition for dissolution of marriage or legal separation of the parties, the husband or wife may bring an action for the exclusive custody of the children of the marriage. The court may, during the pendency of the action, or at the final hearing hereof, or afterwards, make such order regarding the support, care, custody, education, and control of the children of the marriage as may be just and in accordance with the natural rights of the parents and best interest of the children. The order may be modified or terminated at any time thereafter as the natural rights of the parties and the best interest of the children may require.

CHAPTER 8 - LOCATION OF MISSING PARTY OR CHILD

Section 3130   District Attorneys' Duties-Locating Party and Child, Believed Not to Appear
If a petition to determine custody of a child has been filed in a court of competent jurisdiction, or if a temporary order pending determination of custody has been entered in accordance with Chapter 3 (commencing with Section 3060), and the whereabouts of a party in possession of the child are not known, or there is reason to believe that the party may not appear in the proceedings although ordered to appear personally with the child pursuant to Section 3411, the district attorney shall take all actions necessary to locate the party and the child and to procure compliance with the order to appear with the child for purposes of adjudication of custody. The petition to determine custody may be filed by the district attorney.

Section 3131   District Attorneys' Duties-Locating Party and Child in Violation of Court Order and Enforcement of Order
If a custody or visitation order has been entered by a court of competent jurisdiction and the child is taken or detained by another person in violation of the order, the district attorney shall take all actions necessary to locate and return the child and the person who violated the order and to assist in the enforcement of the custody or visitation order or other order of the court by use of an appropriate civil or criminal proceeding.

Section 3132   Scope of District Attorney's Representation
In performing the functions described in Sections 3130 and 313, the district attorney shall act on behalf of the court and shall not represent any party to the custody proceedings.

Section 3133   Temporary Custody Order and Sole Physical Custody Orders
If the district attorney represents to the court, by a written declaration under penalty of perjury that a temporary custody order is needed to recover a child who is being detained or concealed in violation of a court order or a parent's right to custody, the court may issue an order, placing temporary sole physical custody in the parent or person recommended by the district attorney to facilitate the return of the child to the jurisdiction of the court, pending further hearings. If the court determines that it is not in the best interest of the child to place temporary sole physical custody with the parent or person recommended by the district attorney, the court shall appoint a person to take charge of the child and return the child to the jurisdiction of the court.

Section 3134   Order of Payment Of District Attorney's Expenses
(a) When the district attorney incurs expenses pursuant to this chapter, including expenses incurred in a sister state, payment of the expenses may be advanced by the county subject to reimbursement by the state, and shall be audited by the Controller and paid by the State Treasury according to law.
(b) The court in which the custody proceeding is pending or which has continuing jurisdiction shall, if appropriate, allocate liability for the reimbursement of actual expenses incurred by the district attorney to either or both parties to the proceedings and that allocation shall constitute a judgement for the state for the funds advanced pursuant to this section. The county shall take reasonable action to enforce that

liability and shall transmit recovered funds to the state.

Section 3134.5 Protective Custody Warrant

(a) Upon request of the district attorney, the court may issue a protective custody warrant to secure the recovery of an unlawfully detained or concealed child. The request by the district attorney shall include a written declaration under penalty of perjury that a warrant for the child is necessary in order for the district attorney to perform the duties described in Sections 3130 and 3131. The protective custody warrant for the child shall contain an order that the arresting agency shall place the child in protective custody, or return the child as directed by the court. The protective custody warrant may be served in any county in the same manner as a warrant of arrest and may be served at any time of the day or night.

(b) Upon a declaration of the district attorney that the child has been recovered or that the warrant is otherwise no longer required, the court may dismiss the warrant without further court proceedings.

CHAPTER 9 - CHECK TO DETERMINE WHETHER CHILD IS MISSING PERSON

Section 3140 Submission Of Child's Birth Certificate To Court-Parent Fails to Appear

(a) Subject to subdivisions (b) and (c), before granting or modifying a custody order in a case in which one or both parents of the child have not appeared whether personally or by counsel, the court shall require the parent, petitioner, or other party appearing in the case to submit a certified copy of the child's birth certificate to the court. The court or its designee shall forward the certified copy of the birth certificate to the local police or sheriff's department which shall check with the National Crime Information Center Missing Person System to ascertain whether the child has been reported missing or is the victim of an abduction and shall report the results of the check to the court.

(b) If the custody matter before the court also involves a petition for the dissolution of marriage or the adjudication of paternity rights or duties, this section applies only to a case in which there is no proof of personal service of the petition on the absent parent.

(c) For good cause shown, the court may waive the requirements of this section.

CHAPTER 10 - APPOINTMENT OF COUNSEL TO REPRESENT CHILD

Section 3150 Appointment of Private Counsel to Represent Child

(a) If the court determines that it would be in the best interest of the minor child, the court may appoint private counsel to represent the interests of the child in a custody or visitation proceeding.

(b) Upon entering an appearance on behalf of a child pursuant to this chapter, counsel shall continue to represent that child unless relieved by the court upon the substitution of other counsel by the court or for cause.

Section 3151 Duties and Rights of Appointed Counsel

(a) The child's counsel appointed under this chapter is charged with the representation of the child's best interests. The role of the child's counsel is to gather facts that bear on the best interest of the child, and present those facts to the court, including the child's wishes when counsel deems it appropriate for consideration by the court pursuant to Section 3042. The counsel's duties, unless under the circumstances it is inappropriate to exercise the duty, include interviewing the child, reviewing the court files and all accessible relevant records available to both parties, and making any further investigations as the counsel considers necessary to ascertain facts relevant to the custody or visitation hearings.

(b) At the court's request, counsel shall prepare a written statement of issues and contentions setting forth the facts that bear on the best interests of the child. The statement shall set forth a summary of information received by counsel, a list of the sources of information, the results of the counsel's investigation, and such other matters as the court may direct. The statement and issues of contention shall not contain any communication subject to Section 954 of the Evidence Code. The statement of issues and contentions shall be filed with the court and submitted to the parties or their attorneys of record at least 10 days before the hearing, unless the court orders otherwise.

At the court's request, counsel may orally state the wishes of the child if that information is not a privileged communication subject to Section 954 of the Evidence Code, for consideration by the court pursuant to Section 3042. Counsel shall not be called as a witness in the proceeding. Counsel may introduce and examine counsel's own witnesses, present arguments to the court concerning the child's welfare, and participate further in the proceeding to the degree necessary to represent the child adequately. In consultation with representatives of the Family Law Section of the State Bar and the Senate and Assembly Judiciary Committees, the Judicial Council may specify standards for the preparation of the statement of issues and contentions and may promulgate a model statement of issues and contentions, which shall include simple instructions regarding how to subpoena a witness, and a blank subpoena form.

(c) The child's counsel shall have the following rights:

(1) Reasonable access to the child.

(2) Standing to seek affirmative relief on behalf of the child.

(3) Notice of any proceeding, and all phases of that proceeding, including a request for examination affecting the child.

(4) The right to take any action that is available to a party to the proceeding, including, but not limited to, the following: filing pleadings, making evidentiary objections, and presenting evidence and being heard in the proceeding, which may include, but shall not be limited to, presenting motions and orders to show cause, and participating in settlement conferences, trials, seeking writs, appeals, and arbitrations.

(5) Access to the child's medical, dental, mental health, and other health care records, school and educational records, and the right to interview school personnel, caretakers, health care providers, mental health professionals, and others who have assessed the child or provided care to the child. The release of this information to counsel shall not constitute a waiver of the confidentiality of the reports, files, and any disclosed communications. Counsel may interview mediators; however, the provisions of Sections 3177 and 3182 shall apply.

(6) The right to reasonable advance notice of and the right to refuse any physical or psychological examination or evaluation, for purposes of the proceeding, which has not been ordered by the court.

(7) The right to assert or waive any privilege on behalf of the child.

(8) The right to seek independent psychological or physical examination or evaluation of the child for purposes of the pending proceeding, upon approval by the court.

Section 3151.5   Statement of Issues and Contentions

If a child is represented by court appointed counsel, at every hearing in which the court makes a judicial determination regarding custody or visitation, the court shall consider any statement of issues and contentions of the child's counsel. Any party may subpoena as a witness any person listed in the statement of issues and contentions as having provided information to the attorney, but the attorney shall not be called as a witness.

Section 3152   Release and Review of Relevant Reports Concerning Child

(a) The child's counsel may, upon noticed motion to all parties and the local child protective services agency request the court to authorize release of relevant reports or files, concerning the child represented by the counsel, of the relevant local child protective services agency.

(b) The court shall review the reports or files in camera in order to determine whether they are relevant to the pending action and whether and to what extent they should be released to the child's counsel.

(c) Neither the review by the court nor the release to counsel shall constitute a waiver of the confidentiality of the reports and files. Counsel shall not disclose the contents or existence of the reports or files to anyone unless otherwise permitted by law.

Section 3153   Payment of Attorney's Fees for Appointed Counsel

(a) If the court appoints counsel under this chapter to represent the child, counsel shall receive a reasonable sum for compensation and expenses, the amount of which shall be determined by the court. Except as provided in subdivision (b), this amount shall be paid by the parties in the proportions the court deems just.

(b) Upon its own motion or that of a party, the court shall determine whether both parties together are financially unable to pay all or a portion of the cost of counsel appointed pursuant to this chapter, and the portion of the cost of that counsel which the court finds the parties are unable to pay shall be paid by the county. The Judicial Council shall adopt guidelines to assist in determining financial eligibility for county payment of counsel appointed by the court pursuant to this chapter.

CHAPTER 11 - MEDIATION OF VISITATION OR CUSTODY ISSUES

Section 3160   Availability of Mediator by Superior Court

Each superior court shall make a mediator available. The court is not required to institute a family conciliation court in order to provide mediation services.

Section 3161   Purpose Of Mediation Proceedings

The purposes of a mediation proceeding are as follows:

(a) To reduce acrimony that may exist between the parties.

(b) To develop an agreement assuring the child close and continuing contact with both parents that is in the best interest of the child, consistent with Sections 3011 and 3020.

(c) To effect a settlement of the issue of visitation rights of all parties that is in the best interest of the child.

Section 3162   Uniform Standards Of Practice Adopted by Judicial Council

(a) Mediation of cases involving custody and visitation concerning children shall be governed by uniform standards of practice adopted by the Judicial Council.

(b) The standards of practice shall include, but not be limited to, all of the following:

(1) Provision for the best interest of the child and the safeguarding of the rights of the child to frequent and continuing contact with both parents consistent with Sections 3011 and 3020.

(2) Facilitation of the transition of the family by detailing factors to be considered in decisions concerning the child's future.

(3) The conducting of negotiations in such a way as to equalize power relationships between the parties.

(c) In adopting the standards of practice, the Judicial Council shall consider standards developed by recognized associations of mediators and attorneys and other relevant standards governing mediation of proceedings for the dissolution of marriage.

(d) The Judicial Council shall offer training with respect to the standards to mediators.

Section 3163   Adoption of Local Rules to Regulate Mediators

Courts shall develop local rules to respond to requests for a change of mediators or to general problems relating to mediation.

Section 3164   Mediator Qualifications

(a) The mediator may be a member of the professional staff of a family conciliation court, probation department, or mental health services agency, or may be any other person or agency designated by the court.

(b) The mediator shall meet the minimum qualifications required of a counselor of conciliation as provided in Section 1815.

Section 3165   Continuing   Education Requirements

Any person, regardless of administrative title, hired on or after January 1, 1998, who is responsible for clinical supervision of evaluators, investigators, or mediators or who directly supervises or administers the Family Court Services evaluation or mediation programs shall meet the same continuing education requirements specified in Section 1816 for supervising and associate counselors of conciliation.

ARTICLE 2 - AVAILABILITY OF MEDIATION

Section 3170   Setting Matter for Mediation of Contested Issues; Handling of Domestic Violence Cases

(a) If it appears on the face of a petition, application, or other pleading to obtain or modify a temporary or permanent custody or visitation order that custody, visitation, or both are contested, the court shall set the contested issues for mediation.

(b) Domestic violence cases shall be handled by Family Court Services in accordance with a separate written protocol approved by the Judicial Council. The Judicial Council shall adopt guidelines for services, other than services provided under this chapter, that counties may offer to parents who have been unable to resolve their disputes. These services may include, but are not limited to, parent education programs, booklets, videotapes, or referrals to additional communicate resources.

Section 3171   Purpose of Mediation and Party's Involvement

(a) If a stepparent or grandparent has petitioned, or otherwise applied, for a visitation order pursuant to Chapter 5 (commencing with Section 3100), the court shall set the matter for mediation.

(b) A natural or adoptive parent who is not a party to the proceeding is not required to participate in the mediation proceeding, but failure to participate is a waiver of that parent's right to object to a settlement reached by the other parties during mediation or to require a hearing on the matter.

Section 3172   Paternity Not Grounds for Denial of Mediation

Mediation shall not be denied to the parties on the basis that paternity is at issue in a proceeding before the court.

Section 3173   Mediation of Dispute Concerning Existing Order

(a) Upon the adoption of a resolution by the board of supervisors authorizing the procedure, a petition may be filed pursuant to this chapter for mediation of a dispute relating to an existing order for custody, visitation, or both.

(b) The mediation of a dispute concerning an existing order shall be set not later that 60 days after the filing of the petition.

ARTICLE 3 - MEDIATION PROCEEDINGS

Section 3175   Mediation Set Concurrently With Matter for Hearing

If a matter is set for mediation pursuant to this chapter, the mediation shall be set before or concurrent with the setting of the matter for hearing.

Section 3176   Notice Of Mediation

(a) Notice of mediation and of any hearing to be held pursuant to this chapter shall be given to the following persons:

(1) Where mediation is required to settle a contested issue of custody or visitation, to each party and to each party's counsel of record.

(2) Where a stepparent or grandparent seeks visitation rights, to the stepparent or grandparent seeking visitation rights, to each parent of the child, and to each parent's counsel of record.

(b) Notice shall be given by certified mail, return receipt requested, postage prepaid, to the last known address.

Section 3177   Private and Confidential Proceedings

Mediation proceedings pursuant to this chapter shall be held in private and shall be confidential. All communications, verbal or written, from the parties to the mediator made in the proceeding are official information within the meaning of Section 1040 of the Evidence Code.

Section 3178   Limits Of Agreement Reached During Mediation

An agreement reached by the parties as a result of mediation shall be limited as follows:

(a) Where mediation is required to settle a contested issue of custody or visitation, the agreement shall be limited to the resolution of issues relating to parenting plans, custody, visitation, or a combination of these issues.

(b) Where a stepparent or grandparent seeks visitation rights, the agreement shall be limited to the resolution of issues related to visitation.

Section 3179   Modification of Agreement Reached During Mediation

A custody or visitation agreement reached as a result of mediation may be modified at any time at the discretion of the court, subject to Chapter 1 (commencing with Section 3040), Chapter 4 (commencing with Section 3080), and Chapter

5 (commencing with Section 3100).

Section 3180 Duties of Mediator-Protect Interests of Child

(a) In mediation proceedings pursuant to this chapter, the mediator has the duty to assess the needs and interests of the child involved in the controversy, and is entitled to interview the child where the mediator considers the interview appropriate or necessary.

(b) The mediator shall use his or her best efforts to effect a settlement of the custody or visitation dispute that is in the best interest of the child, as provided in Section 3011.

Section 3181 Guidelines for Separate Meetings with Mediator; Intake Forms

(a) In a proceeding in which mediation is required pursuant to this chapter, where there has been a history of domestic violence between the parties or where a protective order as defined in Section 6218 is in effect, at the request of the party alleging domestic violence in a written declaration under penalty of perjury or protected by the order, the mediator appointed pursuant to this chapter shall meet with the parties separately and at separate times.

(b) Any intake form that an agency charged with providing family court services requires the parties to complete before the commencement of mediation shall state that, if a party alleging domestic violence in a written declaration under penalty of perjury or a party protected by a protective order so requests, the mediator will meet with the parties separately and at separate times.

Section 3182 Exclusion of Counsel or Support Person by Mediator

(a) The mediator has authority to exclude counsel from participation in the mediation proceedings pursuant to this chapter if, in the mediator's discretion, exclusion of counsel is appropriate or necessary.

(b) The mediator has authority to exclude a domestic violence support person from a mediation proceeding as provided in Section 6303.

Section 3183 M e d i a t o r ' s Recommendations To Court-Child Custody,

Visitation, etc.

(a) The mediator may, consistent with local court rules, submit a recommendation to the court as to the custody of or visitation with the child.

(b) Where the parties have not reached an agreement as a result of the mediation proceedings, the mediator may recommend to the court that an investigation be conducted pursuant to Chapter 6 (commencing with Section 3110) or that other services be offered to assist the parties to effect a resolution of the controversy before a hearing on the issues.

(c) In appropriate cases, the mediator may recommend that restraining orders be issued, pending determination of the controversy, to protect the well-being of the child involved in the controversy.

Section 3184 Mediator's Recommendations for Appointed Counsel for Minor

Nothing in this chapter prohibits the mediator from recommending to the court that counsel be appointed, pursuant to Chapter 10 (commencing with Section 3150), to represent the minor child. In making this recommendation, the mediator shall inform the court of the reasons why it would be in the best interest of the minor child to have counsel appointed.

Section 3185 Mediator's Recommendation to Court-Unresolved Issues

(a) If issues that may be resolved by agreement pursuant to Section 3178 are not resolved by an agreement of all the parties who participate in mediation, the mediator shall inform the court in writing and the court shall set the matter for hearing on the unresolved issues.

(b) Where a stepparent or grandparent requests visitation each natural or adoptive parent and the stepparent or grandparent shall be given an opportunity to appear and be heard on the issue visitation.

Section 3186 Guidelines for Agreement Reached Through Mediation

(a) An agreement reached by the parties as a result of mediation shall be reported to counsel for the parties by the mediator on the day set for mediation or as soon thereafter as practical, but before the agreement is reported to the court.

(b) An agreement may not be confirmed or

otherwise incorporated in an order unless each party, in person or be counsel of record, has affirmed and assented to the agreement in open court or by written stipulation.

(c) An agreement may be confirmed or otherwise incorporated in an order if a party fails to appear at a noticed hearing on the issue involved in the agreement.

CHAPTER 12 - COUNSELING OF PARENTS AND CHILD

Section 3190   Court Grounds for Ordering Counseling

(a) The court may require parents involved in a custody or visitation dispute, and the minor child, to participate in outpatient counseling with a licensed mental health professional, or through other community programs and services that provide appropriate counseling, including, but not limited to, mental health or substance abuse services, for not more than one year, provided that the program selected has counseling available for the designated period of time, if the court finds both of the following:

(1) The dispute between the parents or between a parent and the child poses a substantial danger to the best interest of the child.

(2) The counseling is in the best interest of the child.

(b) Subject to Section 3192, if the court finds that the financial burden created by the order for counseling does not otherwise jeopardize a party's other financial obligations, the court shall fix the cost and shall order the entire cost of the services to be borne by the parties in the proportions the court deems reasonable.

(c) The court, in its ruling, shall set forth reasons why it has found both of the following:

(1) The dispute poses a substantial danger to the best interest of the child and the counseling is in the best interest of the child.

(2) The financial burden created by the court order for counseling does not otherwise jeopardize a party's other financial obligations.

(d) The court shall not order the parties to return to court upon the completion of counseling. Either party may file a new order to show cause or motion after counseling has been completed, and the court may again order counseling consistent with this chapter.

Section 3191   Purpose of Counseling

The counseling pursuant to this chapter shall be specifically designed to facilitate communication between the parties regarding their minor child's best interest, to reduce conflict regarding custody or visitation, and to improve the quality of parenting skills of each parent.

Section 3192   Separate Counseling Sessions- History of Domestic Violence

In a proceeding in which counseling is ordered pursuant to this chapter, where there has been history of abuse by either parent against the child or by one parent against the other parent and a protective order as defined in Section 6218 is in effect, the court may order the parties to participate in counseling separately, unless good cause is shown for a different apportionment. The costs associated with a minor child participating in counseling shall be apportioned in accordance with Section 4062.

CHAPTER 13 - SUPERVISED VISITATION

Section 3200   Development of Standards for Supervised Visitation

The Judicial Council shall develop standards for supervised visitation providers in accordance with the guidelines set forth in this action. On or before April 1, 1997, the Judicial Council shall report the standards developed and present an implementation plan to the Legislature. For the purposes of the development of these standards, the term "provider" shall include any individual who functions as a visitation monitor, as well as supervised visitation centers. Provisions shall be made within the standards to allow for the diversity of supervised visitation providers.

(a) When developing standards, the Judicial Council shall consider all of the following issues:

(1) The providers' qualifications, experience, and education.

(2) Safety and security procedures, including ratios of children per supervisor.

(3) Any conflict of interest.

(4) Maintenance and disclosure of records, including confidentiality policies.

(5) Procedures for screening, delineation of terms and conditions, and termination of supervised visitation services.

(6) Procedures for emergency or

extenuating situations.

(7) Orientation to and guidelines for cases in which there are allegation of domestic violence, child abuse, substance abuse, or special circumstances.

(8) The legal obligations and responsibilities of supervisors.

(b) The Judicial Council shall consult with visitation centers, mothers' groups, fathers' groups, judges, the State Bar of California, children's advocacy groups, domestic violence prevention groups, Family Court Services, and other groups it regards as necessary in connection with these standards.

(c) It is the intent of the legislature that the safety of children, adults, and visitation supervisors be a precondition to providing visitation services. Once safety is assured, the best interest of the child is the paramount consideration at all stages and particularly in deciding the manner in which supervision is provided.

PART 3 - UNIFORM CHILD CUSTODY JURISDICTION ACT

Section 3400   Citation for Title
This part may be cited as the Uniform Child custody Jurisdiction Act.

Section 3401   Purposes of Part
(a) The general purposes of this part are to:

(1) Avoid jurisdiction competition and conflict with courts of other states in matters of child custody which have in the past resulted in the shifting of children from state to state with harmful effects on their well-being.

(2) Promote cooperation with the courts of other states to the end that a custody decree is rendered in that state which can best decide the case in the interest of the child.

(3) Assure that litigation concerning the custody of child take place ordinarily in the state with which the child and the child's family have the closest connection and where significant evidence concerning the child's care, protection, training, and personal relationships is most readily available, and that courts of this state decline the exercise of jurisdiction when the child and the child's family have a closer connection with another state.

(4) Discourage continuing controversies

over child custody in the interest of greater stability of home environment and of secure family relationships for the child.

(5) Deter abductions and other unilateral removals of children undertaken to obtain custody awards.

(6) Avoid relitigation of custody decisions of other states in this state insofar as feasible.

(7) Facilitate the enforcement of custody decrees of other states.

(8) Promote and expand the exchange of information and other forms of mutual assistance between the courts of this state and those of other states concerned with the same child.

(b) This part shall be construed to promote the general purposes stated in this section.

Section 3402   Definitions
As used in this part:

(a) "Contestant" means a person, including a parent, who claims a right to custody visitation rights with respect to a child.

(b) "Custody determination" means a court decision and court orders and instructions providing for the custody of a child, including visitation rights; it does not include a decision relating to child support or any other monetary obligation of any person.

(c) "Custody proceeding" includes proceedings in which a custody determination is one of several issues, such as a proceeding for dissolution of marriage or for legal separation of the parties, and includes child neglect and dependency proceedings.

(d) "Decree" or "custody decree" means a custody determination contained in a judicial decree or order made in a custody proceeding, and includes an initial decree and a modification decree.

(e) "Home state" means the state in which the child immediately preceding the time involved lived with the child's parents, a parent, or a person acting as parent, for at least six consecutive months, and in the case of a child less than six months old the state in which the child lived from birth with any of the persons mentioned. Periods of temporary absence of any of the named persons are counted as part of the six-month or other period.

(f) "Initial decree" means the first custody decree concerning a particular child.

(g) "Modification decree" means a custody

decree which modifies or replaces a prior decree, whether made by the court which rendered the prior decree or by another court.

(h) "Physical custody" means actual possession and control of a child.

(i) "Person acting as parent" means a person, other than a parent, who has physical custody of a child and who has either been awarded custody by the court or claims a right to custody.

(j) "State" means any state, territory, or possession of the United States, the Commonwealth of Puerto Rico, and the District of Columbia.

Section 3403   Conditions for Jurisdiction

(a) A court of this state which is competent to decide child custody matters has jurisdiction to make a child custody determination by initial or modification decree if the conditions as set forth in any of the following paragraphs are met:

(1) This state (A) is the home state for the child at the time of commencement of the proceeding, or (B) had been the child's home state within six months before commencement of the proceeding and the child is absent from this state because of removal or retention by a person claiming custody of the child or for other reasons, and a parent or person acting as parent continues to live in this state.

(2) It is in the best interest of the child that a court of this state assume jurisdiction because (A) the child and the child's parents, or the child and at least one contestant, have significant connection with this state, and (B) there is available in this state substantial evidence concerning the child's present or future care, protection, training, and personal relationships.

(3) The child is physically present in this state and (A) the child has been abandoned or (B) it is necessary in an emergency to protect the child because the child has been subjected to or threatened with mistreatment or abuse or is otherwise neglected or dependent. For the purposes of this subdivision, "subjected to or threatened with mistreatment or abuse" includes a child who has a parent who is a victim of domestic violence, as defined in Section 6211.

(4) Both of the following conditions are satisfied:

(A) It appears that no other state would

have jurisdiction under prerequisites substantially in accordance with paragraph (1), (2), or (3) or another state has declined to exercise jurisdiction on the ground that this state is the more appropriate forum to determine the custody of the child.

(B) It is in the best interest of the child that this court assume jurisdiction.

(b) Except under the conditions specified in paragraphs (3) and (4) of subdivision (a), physical presence in this state of the child, or of the child and one of the contestants, is not alone sufficient to confer jurisdiction on a court of this state to make a child custody determination.

(c) Physical presence of the child, while desirable, is not a prerequisite for jurisdiction to determine the custody of the child.

Section 3404   Reasonable Notice and Opportunity to Be Heard-Parent, Person with Custody

Before making a decree under this part, reasonable notice and opportunity to be heard shall be given to the contestants, any parent whose parental rights have not been previously terminated, and any person who has physical custody of the child. If any of these persons is outside this state, notice and opportunity to be heard shall be given pursuant to Section 3405.

Section 3405   Service of Notice to Persons Out-of-State

(a) Notice required for the exercise of jurisdiction over a person outside this state shall be given in a manner reasonably calculated to give actual notice, and may be made in any of the following ways:

(1) By personal delivery outside this state in the manner prescribed for service of process within this state.

(2) In the manner prescribed by the law of the place in which the service is made for service of process in that place in an action in any of its courts of general jurisdiction.

(3) By any form of mail addressed to the person to be served and requesting a receipt.

(4) As directed by the court (including publication, if other means of notification are ineffective).

(b) Notice under this section shall be served, mailed delivered, or last published at least 10 days before any hearing in this state.

(c) Proof of service outside this state may be made by affidavit of the individual who made the service, or in the manner prescribed by the law of this state, the order pursuant to which the service is made, or the law of the place in which the service is made. If service is made by mail, proof may be a receipt signed by the addressee or other evidence of delivery to the addressee.

(d) Notice is not required if a person submits to the jurisdiction of the court.

Section 3406   Jurisdiction During Pendency of Proceeding in Other State

(a) A court of this state shall not exercise its jurisdiction under this part if at the time of filing the petition a proceeding concerning the custody of the child was pending in a court of another state exercising jurisdiction substantially in conformity with this part, unless the proceeding is stayed by the court of the other state because this state is a more appropriate forum or for other reasons.

(b) Before hearing the petition in a custody proceeding, the court shall examine the pleadings and other information supplied by the parties under Section 3410 and shall consult the child custody registry established under Section 3417 concerning the pendency of proceedings with respect to the child in other states. If the court has reason to believe that proceedings may be pending in another state, it shall direct an inquiry to the state court administrator or other appropriate official of the other state.

(c) If the court is informed during the course of the proceeding that a proceeding concerning the custody of the child was pending in another state before the court assumed jurisdiction, it shall stay the proceeding and communicate with the court in which the other proceeding is pending to the end that the issue may be litigated in the more appropriate forum and that information be exchanged in accordance with Sections 3420 to 3423, inclusive. If a court of this state has made a custody decree before being informed of a pending proceeding in a court of another state, it shall immediately inform that court of the fact. If the court is informed that a proceeding was commenced in another state after it assumed jurisdiction, it shall likewise inform the other court to the end that the issues may be litigated in the more appropriate forum.

Section 3407   Exercise of Jurisdiction After Finding of Inconvenient Forum

(a) A court which has jurisdiction under this part to make an initial or modification decree may decline to exercise its jurisdiction any time before making a decree if it finds that is an inconvenient forum to make a custody determination under the circumstances of the case and that a court of another state is a more appropriate forum.

(b) A finding of inconvenient forum may be made upon the court's own motion or upon motion of a party or a guardian ad litem or other representative of the child.

(c) In determining if it is an inconvenient forum, the court shall consider if it is in the interest of the child that another state assume jurisdiction. For this purpose it may take into account the following factors, among others;

(1) If another state is or recently was the child's home state.

(2) If another state has a closer connection with the child and the child's family or with the child and one or more of the contestants.

(3) If substantial evidence concerning the child's recent or future care, protection, training and personal relationships is more readily available in another state.

(4) If the parties have agreed on another forum which is no less appropriate.

(5) If the exercise of jurisdiction by a court of this state would contravene any of the purposes stated in Section 3401.

(d) Before determining whether to decline or retain jurisdiction, the court may communicate with a court of another state and exchange information pertinent to the assumption of jurisdiction by either court with a view to ensuring that jurisdiction will be exercised by the more appropriate court and that a forum will be available to the parties.

(e) If the court finds that it is an inconvenient forum and that a court of another state is a more appropriate forum, it may dismiss the proceedings, or it may stay the proceedings upon condition that a custody proceeding be promptly commenced in another named state or upon any other conditions which may be just and proper, including the condition that a moving party stipulate consent and submission to the jurisdiction of the other forum.

(f) The court may decline to exercise its jurisdiction under this part if a custody determination is incidental to an action for divorce or another proceeding while retaining jurisdiction over the divorce or other proceeding.

(g) If it appears to the court that it is clearly an inappropriate forum, the court may require the party who commenced the proceedings to pay in addition to the costs of the proceedings in this state, necessary travel and other expenses, including attorney's fees, incurred by other parties or their witnesses. Payment is to be made to the clerk of the court for remittance to the proper party.

(h) Upon dismissal or stay of proceedings under this section, the court shall inform the court found to be the more appropriate forum of this fact, or if the court which would have jurisdiction in the other state is not certainly known, shall transmit the information to the court administrator or other appropriate official for forwarding to the appropriate court.

(i) Any communication received from another state informing this state of a findings of inconvenient forum shall be filed in the custody registry of the appropriate court. Upon assuming jurisdiction, the court of this state shall inform the original court of this fact.

Section 3408   Jurisdiction Declined Due to Prior Reprehensible Conduct

(a) If the petitioner for an initial decree has wrongfully taken the child from another state or has engaged in similar reprehensible conduct, the court may decline to exercise jurisdiction for purposes of adjudication of custody if this is just and proper under the circumstances.

(b) Unless required in the interest of the child, the court shall not exercise its jurisdiction to modify a custody decree of another state if the petitioner, without consent of the person entitled to custody, has improperly removed the child from the physical custody of the person entitled to custody or has improperly retained the child after a visit or other temporary relinquishment of physical custody. If the petitioner has violated any other provision of a custody decree of another state, the court may decline to exercise its jurisdiction if this is just and proper under the circumstances.

(c) Where the court declines to exercise jurisdiction upon petition for an initial custody decree pursuant to subdivision (a), the court shall notify the parent or other appropriate person and the prosecuting attorney of the appropriate jurisdiction in the other state. If a request to that effect is received from the other state, the court shall order the petitioner to appear with the child in a custody proceeding instituted in the other state in accordance with Section 3421. If no request is made within a reasonable time after the notification, the court may entertain a petition to determine custody by the petitioner if it has jurisdiction pursuant to Section 3403.

(d) Where the court refuses to assume jurisdiction to modify the custody decree of another state pursuant to subdivision (b) or pursuant to Section 3414, the court shall notify the person who has legal custody under the decree of the other state and the prosecuting attorney of the appropriate jurisdiction in the other state and may order the petitioner to return the child to the person who has legal custody. If it appears that the order will be ineffective and the legal custodian is ready to receive the child within a period of a few days, the court may place the child in a foster care home for that period, pending return of the child to the legal custodian. At the same time, the court shall advise the petitioner that any petition for modification of custody must be directed to (1) the appropriate court of the other state which has continuing jurisdiction or (2) if that court declines jurisdiction, to a court in a state which has jurisdiction pursuant to Section 3403.

(e) In appropriate cases, a court dismissing a petition under this section may charge the petitioner with necessary travel and other expenses, including attorney's fees and the cost of returning the child to another state.

(f) In making a determination pursuant to subdivisions (a) to (e), inclusive, the court shall not consider as a factor weighing against the petitioner any taking of the child, or retention of the child after a visit or other temporary relinquishment of physical custody, from the person who has legal custody, if there is evidence that the taking or retention of the child was a result of domestic violence against the petitioner, as defined in Section 6211.

Section 3409   Information on First Pleading
or Affidavit from Every Party
(a) Every party in a custody proceeding in the party's first pleading or in an affidavit attached to that pleading shall give information under oath as to the child's present address, the places where the child has lived within the last five years, and the names and present addresses of the persons with whom the child has lived during that period. However, where there are allegations of domestic violence or child abuse, any addresses of the party alleging abuse and of the child that are unknown to the other party are confidential and may not be disclosed in the pleading or affidavit. In this pleading or affidavit, every party shall further declare under oath as to each of the following whether the party:

(1) Has participated, as a party, witness, or in any other capacity, in any other litigation concerning the custody of the same child in this or any other state.

(2) Has information of any custody proceeding concerning the child pending in a court of this or any other state.

(3) Knows of any person not a party to the proceedings who has physical custody of the child or claims to have custody or visitation rights with respect to the child.

(b) If the declaration as to any of the above items is in the affirmative, the declarant shall give additional information under oath as required by the court. The court may examine the parties under oath as to details of the information furnished and as to other matters pertinent to the court's jurisdiction and the disposition of the case.

(c) Each party has a continuing duty to inform the court of any custody proceeding concerning the child in this or any other state of which the party obtained information during this proceeding.

Section 3410   Joinder of Person With
Custody of Child
If the court learns from information furnished by the parties pursuant to Section 3409 or from other sources that a person not a party to the custody proceeding has physical custody of the child or claims to have custody or visitation rights with respect to the child, it shall order that person to be joined as a party and to be

duly notified of the pendency of the proceeding and of the person's joinder as a party. If the person joined as a party is outside this state, the person shall be served with process or otherwise notified in accordance with Section 3405.

Section 3411   Orders to Appear
(a) The court may order any party to the proceeding who is with or without the child to appear personally before the court. If that party has physical custody of the child, the court may order him or her to appear personally with the child. If the party who is ordered to appear with the child cannot be served or fails to obey the order, or it appears the order will be ineffective, the court may issue a warrant of arrest against the party and a protective custody warrant for the child, to secure the party's or the child's appearance or both, before the court. The protective custody warrant for the child shall contain an order that the arresting agency shall place the child in protective custody, or return the child as directed by the court. The protective custody warrant may be served in any county in the same manner as a warrant of arrest and may be served at any time of the day or night.
(b) If a party to the proceeding whose presence is desired by the court is outside this state with or without the child the court may order that the notice given under Section 3405 include a statement directing that party to appear personally with or without the child and stating that failure to appear may result in a decision adverse to that party and the issuance of a warrant pursuant to subdivision (a).
(c) If a party to the proceeding who is outside this state is directed to appear under subdivision (b) or desires to appear personally before the court with or without the child, the court may require another party to pay to the clerk of the court travel and other necessary expenses of the party so appearing and of the child if this is just and proper under the circumstances.

Section 3412   Custody Decree as Binding
and Conclusive
A custody decree rendered by a court of this state which had jurisdiction under Section 3403 binds all parties who have been served in this state or notified in accordance with Section 3405 or who have submitted to the jurisdiction of the court, and who have been given an opportunity to be

heard. As to these parties, the custody decree is conclusive as to all issues of law and fact decided and as to the custody determination made unless and until that determination is modified pursuant to law, including this part.

Section 3413   Recognition   and Enforcement of Out-Of-State Custody Decree
The courts of this state shall recognize and enforce an initial or modification decree of a court of another state which had assumed jurisdiction under statutory provisions substantially in accordance with this part or which was made under factual circumstances meeting the jurisdictional standards of this part, so long as this decree has not been modified in accordance with jurisdictional standards substantially similar to those of this part.

Section 3414   Modification of Custody Decree Of Another State
(a) If a court of another state has made a custody decree, a court of this state shall not modify that decree unless (1) it appears to the court of this state that the court which rendered the decree does not now have jurisdiction under jurisdictional prerequisites substantially in accordance with this part or has declined to assume jurisdiction to modify the decree and (2) the court of this state has jurisdiction.
(b) If a court of this state is authorized under subdivision (a) and Section 3408 to modify a custody decree of another state, the court shall give due consideration to the transcript of the record and other documents of all previous proceedings submitted to it in accordance with Section 3423.

Section 3415   Application of Section 3140.
Section 3140 is applicable to proceedings pursuant to this part.

Section 3416   Filing and Enforcement of Out-of-State Custody Decree
(a) A certified copy of a custody decree of another state may be filed in the office of the clerk of any superior court of this state. The clerk shall treat the decree in the same manner as a custody decree of the superior court of this state. A custody decree so filed has the same effect and shall be enforced in like manner as a custody decree rendered by a court of this state.

(b) A person violating a custody decree of another state which makes it necessary to enforce the decree in this state may be required to pay necessary travel and other expenses, including attorney's fees, incurred by the party entitled to the custody or that party's witness.

Section 3417   Superior Court Clerk to Maintain Registry of Out-of-State Custody Decrees
The clerk of each superior court shall maintain a registry in which the clerk shall enter all of the following:
(a) Certified copies of custody decrees of other states received for filing.
(b) Communications as to the pendency of custody proceedings in other states.
(c) Communications concerning a finding of inconvenient forum by a court of another state.
(d) Other communications or documents concerning custody proceedings in another state which may affect the jurisdiction of a court of this state or the disposition to be made by it in a custody proceeding.
(e) Any custody agreement for which an order is requested regarding a child who is not the subject of another order. The parties shall submit the affidavit required by Section 3409, on the form developed by the Judicial Council for use with Section 3409.

Section 3418   Forwarding Certified Copies of Custody Decree by Clerk
The clerk of a superior court of this state, at the request of the court of another state or at the request of any person who is affected by or has a legitimate interest in a custody decree, shall certify and forward a copy of the decree to that court or person.

Section 3419   Testimony of Out-of-State Witnesses
In addition to other procedural devices available to a party, any party to the proceeding or a guardian ad litem, or other representative of the child may adduce testimony of witnesses, including parties and the child, by deposition or otherwise, in another state. The court on its own motion may direct that the testimony of a person be taken in another state and may prescribe the manner in which and the terms upon which the testimony shall be taken.

Section 3420   Request for Another State's Courts to Obtain Evidence, Social Studies, Order of Personal Appearance

(a) A court of this state may request the appropriate court of another state to hold a hearing to adduce evidence, to order a party to produce or give evidence under other procedures of that state, or to have social studies made with respect to the custody of a child involved in proceedings pending in the court of this state; and to forward to the court of this state certified copies of the transcript of the record of the hearing, the evidence otherwise adduced, or any social studies prepared in compliance with the request. The cost of the services may be assessed against the parties or, if necessary, ordered paid by the state.

(b) A court of this state may request the appropriate court of another state to order a party to custody proceedings pending in the court of this state to appear in the proceedings, and if that party has physical custody of the child, to appear with the child. The request may state that travel and other necessary expenses of the party and of the child whose appearance is desired will be assessed against another party or will otherwise be paid.

Section 3421   Action on Another State's Request for Evidence, Order for Personal Appearance

(a) Upon request of the court of another state, the courts of this state which are competent to hear custody matters may order a person in this state to appear at a hearing to adduce evidence or to produce or give evidence under other procedures available in this state. A certified copy of the transcript of the record of the hearing or the evidence otherwise adduced shall be forwarded by the clerk of the court to the requesting court.

(b) A person within this state may voluntarily give his or her testimony or statement in this state for use in a custody proceeding outside this state.

(c) Upon request of the court of another state, a competent court of this state may order a person in this state to appear alone or with the child in a custody proceeding in another state. The court may condition compliance with the request upon assurance by the other state that travel and other necessary expenses will be advanced or reimbursed. If the person who has physical custody of the child cannot be served or fails to obey the order, or it appears the order will be ineffective, the court may issue a warrant of arrest against the person to secure the person's appearance with the child in the other state.

Section 3422   Preservation of Records; Forwarding to Another State.

In any custody proceeding in this state, the court shall preserve the pleadings, orders and decrees, any record that has been made of its hearings, social studies, and other pertinent documents until the child reaches 18 years of age. Upon appropriate request of the court of another state, the court shall forward to the other court certified copies of any or all of such documents.

Section 3423   Request for Certified Copies of Transcripts and Papers in Out-of-State Proceeding

If a custody decree has been rendered in another state concerning a child involved in a custody proceeding pending in a court of this state, the court of this state upon taking jurisdiction of the case shall request of the court of the other state a certified copy of the transcript of any court record and other documents mentioned in Section 3422.

Section 3423   Extension of Policies to International Areas

The general policies of this part extend to the international area. The provisions of this part relating to the recognition and enforcement of custody decrees involving legal institutions similar in nature to custody rendered by appropriate authorities of other nations if reasonable notice and opportunity to be heard were given to all affected persons.

Section 3425   Jurisdictional Questions to Be Handled Expeditiously

Upon the request of a party to a custody proceeding which raises a question of existence or exercise of jurisdiction under this part, the case shall be given calendar priority and handled expeditiously.

ADOPTION STATUTE

Section 8714.5   Adoption   By   Relative:
Legislative Intent
(a) The Legislature finds and declares the following:
(1) It is the intent of the Legislature to expedite legal permanency for children who cannot return to their parents and to remove barriers to adoption by relatives of children who are already in the dependency system or who are at risk of entering the dependency system.
(2) This goal will be achieved by empowering families, including extended families, to care for their own children safely and permanently whenever possible, by preserving existing family relationships, thereby causing the least amount of disruption to the child and the family, and by recognizing the importance of sibling and half-sibling relationships.
(b) A relative desiring to adopt a child may for that purpose file a petition in the county in which the petitioner resides. Where a child has been adjudged to be a dependent of the juvenile court pursuant to Section 300 of the Welfare and Institutions Code, and thereafter has been freed for adoption by the juvenile court, the petition may be filed either in the county where the petitioner resides or in the county where the child was freed for adoption.
(c) Upon the filing of a petition for adoption by a relative, the county clerk shall immediately notify the State Department of Social Services in Sacramento in writing of the pendency of the proceeding and of any subsequent action taken.
(d) If the adopting relative has entered into a kinship adoption agreement with the birth parent as set forth in Section 8714.7, the kinship adoption agreement, signed by the parties to the agreement, shall be attached to and filed with the petition for adoption under subdivision (b).
(e) The caption of the adoption petition shall contain the name of the relative petitioner. The petition shall state the child's name, sex, and date of birth.
(f) If the child is the subject of a guardianship petition, the adoption petition shall so state and shall include the caption and docket number or have attached a copy of the letters of guardianship or temporary guardianship. The petitioner shall notify the court of any petition for adoption. The guardianship proceeding shall be consolidated with the adoption proceeding.
(g) The order of adoption shall contain the child's adopted name and, if requested by the adopting relative, or if requested by the child who is 12 years of age or older, the name the child had before adoption.

Section 8714.7   Kinship Adoption: Agreement For Continuing Contact With Birth Relatives
(a) Nothing in the adoption laws of this state shall be construed to prevent the adopting parent or parents, the birth relatives, including the birth parent or parents, and the child from entering into a written agreement to permit continuing contact between the birth relatives, including the birth parent or parents, and the child if the agreement is found by the court to be in the best interests of the child at the time the adoption petition is granted. The terms of any kinship adoption agreement executed under this section shall be limited to, but need not include, all of the following:
(1) Provisions for visitation between the child and a birth parent or parents and other birth relatives, including siblings.
(2) Provisions for future contact between a birth parent or parents or other birth relatives, including siblings, or both, and the child or an adoptive parent or both.
(3) Provisions for the sharing of information about the child in the future.
(b) At the time an adoption decree is entered pursuant to a petition filed under Section 8714.5, the court entering the decree may grant post adoption privileges when an agreement for those privileges has been entered into pursuant to subdivision (a).
(c) This section is applicable only to kinship adoption agreements in which the adopting parent is a relative of the child or a relative to the child's half-sibling and the adoption petition is filed under Section 8714.5. For purposes of this section and Section 8714.5, "relative" means an adult who is related to the child or the child's half-sibling by blood or affinity, including all relatives whose status is preceded by the words "step," "great," "great-great," or "grand," or the spouse of any of these persons, even if the marriage was terminated by death or dissolution.
(d) The child who is the subject of the adoption petition shall be considered a party to the kinship

adoption agreement. The written consent to the terms and conditions of the kinship adoption agreement and any subsequent modifications of the agreement by a child who is 12 years of age and older is a necessary condition to the granting of privileges regarding visitation, contact, or sharing of information about the child, unless the court finds by a preponderance of the evidence that the agreement, as written, is in the best interests of the child. Any child who has been found to come within Section 300 of the Welfare and Institutions Code or who is the subject of a petition for jurisdiction of the juvenile court under Section 300 of the Welfare and Institutions Code shall be represented by an attorney for purposes of consent to the kinship adoption agreement.

(e)   A kinship adoption agreement shall contain the following warnings in bold type:

(1)   After the adoption petition has been granted by the court, the adoption cannot be set aside due to the failure of an adopting parent, a birth parent, a birth relative, or the child to follow the terms of this agreement or a later change to this agreement.

(2)   A disagreement between the parties or litigation brought to enforce or modify the agreement shall not affect the validity of the adoption and shall not serve as a basis for orders affecting the custody of the child.

(3)   A court will not act on a petition to change or enforce this agreement unless the petitioner has participated, or attempted to participate, in good faith in mediation or other appropriate dispute resolution proceedings to resolve the dispute.

(f)   Upon the granting of the adoption petition and the issuing of the order of adoption of a child who is a dependent of the juvenile court, juvenile court dependency jurisdiction shall be terminated.   Enforcement of the kinship adoption agreement shall be under the continuing jurisdiction of the court granting the petition of adoption. The court may not order compliance with the agreement absent a finding that the party seeking the enforcement participated, or attempted to participate, in good faith in mediation or other appropriate dispute resolution proceedings regarding the conflict, prior to the filing of the enforcement action, and that the enforcement is in the best interests of the child.   Documentary evidence or offers of

proof may serve as the basis for the court's decision regarding enforcement.   No testimony or evidentiary hearing shall be required.   The court shall not order further investigation or evaluation by any public or private agency or individual absent a finding by clear and convincing evidence that the best interests of the child may be protected or advanced only by such inquiry and that the inquiry will not disturb the stability of the child's home to the detriment of the child.

(g)   The court may not award monetary damages as a result of the filing of the civil action pursuant to subdivision (f) of this section.

(h)   A kinship adoption agreement may be modified or terminated only if either of the following occurs:

(1)   All parties, including the child if the child is 12 years of age or older at the time of the requested termination or modification, have signed a modified kinship adoption agreement and the agreement is filed with the court that granted the petition of adoption.

(2)   The court finds all of the following:

(A)   The termination or modification is necessary to serve the best interests of the child.

(B)   There has been a substantial change of circumstances since the original agreement was executed and approved by the court.

(C)   The party seeking the termination or modification has participated, or attempted to participate, in good faith in mediation or other appropriate dispute resolution proceedings prior to seeking court approval of the proposed termination or modification.

Documentary evidence or offers of proof may serve as the basis for the court's decision.   No testimony or evidentiary hearing shall be required.   The court shall not order further investigation or evaluation by any public or private agency or individual absent a finding by clear and convincing evidence that the best interests of the child may be protected or advanced only by such inquiry and that the inquiry will not disturb the stability of the child's home to the detriment of the child.

(i)   All costs and fees of mediation or other appropriate dispute resolution proceedings shall be borne by each party, excluding the child. All costs and fees of litigation shall be borne by the party filing the action to modify or enforce the agreement when no party has been found by the court as failing to comply with an existing kinship adoption agreement. Otherwise, a party, other than the child, found by the court as failing to comply without good cause with an existing agreement shall bear all the costs and fees of litigation.

(j) By July 1, 1998, the Judicial Council shall adopt rules of court and forms for motions to enforce, terminate, or modify kinship adoption agreements.

(k) The court shall not set aside a decree of adoption, rescind a relinquishment, or modify any order to terminate parental rights or any other prior court order because of the failure of a birth parent, adoptive parent, birth relative, or the child to comply with any or all of the original terms of, or subsequent modifications to, the kinship adoption agreement.

Section 8715   Department Or Agency To File Report

The department or licensed adoption agency, whichever is a party to or joins in the petition, shall submit a full report of the facts of the case to the court. Where a petition for adoption by a relative has been filed with a kinship adoption agreement pursuant to Section 8714.7, the report shall address whether the kinship adoption agreement is in the best interests of the child who is the subject of the petition. The department may also submit a report in those cases in which a licensed adoption agency is a party or joins in the adoption petition.

Section 8802   Petition

(a) (1)   Any of the following persons who desire to adopt a child may, for that purpose, file a petition in the county in which the petitioner resides:

(A) A grandparent, aunt, uncle, first cousin, or sibling.

(B) A person named in the will of a deceased parent as an intended adoptive parent where the child has no other parent.

(C) A person with whom a child has been placed for adoption.

(D) A legal guardian who has been the child's legal guardian for more than one year. However, if the parent nominated the guardian for a purpose other than adoption for a specified time period, or if the guardianship was established pursuant to Section 360 of the Welfare and Institutions Code, the guardianship shall have been in existence for not less than three years.

(2)   If the child has been placed for adoption, a copy of the adoptive placement agreement shall be attached to the petition. The court clerk shall immediately notify the department in Sacramento in writing of the pendency of the proceeding and of any subsequent action taken.

(b)   The petition shall contain an allegation that the petitioners will file promptly with the department or delegated county adoption agency information required by the department in the investigation of the proposed adoption. The omission of the allegation from a petition does not affect the jurisdiction of the court to proceed or the validity of an adoption order or other order based on the petition.

(c)   The caption of the adoption petition shall contain the names of the petitioners, but not the child's name. The petition shall state the child's sex and date of birth and the name the child had before adoption.

(d)   If the child is the subject of a guardianship petition, the adoption petition shall so state and shall include the caption and docket number or have attached a copy of the letters of the guardianship or temporary guardianship. The petitioners shall notify the court of any petition for guardianship or temporary guardianship filed after the adoption petition. The guardianship proceeding shall be consolidated with the adoption proceeding.

(e)   The order of adoption shall contain the child's adopted name, but not the name the child had before adoption.

(f)   This section shall become operative on January 1, 1995.

PERSONAL NOTES:

WELFARE & INSTITUTIONS CODE SECTION 360
DISPOSITION ORDERS

After receiving and considering the evidence on the proper disposition of the case, the juvenile court may enter judgment as follows:

(A) Notwithstanding any other provision of law, if the court finds that the minor is a person described by Section 300 and the parent has advised the court that the parent is not interested in family maintenance or family reunification services, it may, in addition to or in lieu of adjudicating the minor a dependent child of the court, order a legal guardianship, appoint a legal guardian, and issue letters of guardianship, if the court determines that a guardianship is in the best interest of the minor, provided the parent and the minor agree to the guardianship, unless the minor's age or physical, emotional, or mental condition prevents the minor's meaningful response. The court shall advise the parent and the minor that no reunification services will be provided as a result of the establishment of a guardianship. The proceeding for the appointment of a guardian shall be in the juvenile court.

Any application for termination of guardianship shall be filed in juvenile court in a form as may be developed by the Judicial Council pursuant to Section 68511 of the Government Code. Section 388 shall apply to this order of guardianship.

No person shall be appointed a legal guardian under this section until an assessment as specified in subdivision (g) of Section 361.5 is read and considered by the court and reflected in the minutes of the court. The assessment shall include the following:

1. Current search efforts for, and notification of, a noncustodial parent in the manner provided in Section 337.

2. A review of the amount of and nature of any contact between the minor and his or her parents since the filing of the petition.

3. An evaluation of the minor's medical, developmental, scholastic, mental, and emotional status.

4. A preliminary assessment of the eligibility and commitment of any identified prospective guardian, particularly the caretaker, to include a

social history including a screening for criminal records and prior referrals for child abuse or neglect, the capability to meet the minor's needs, and the understanding of the legal and financial rights and responsibilities of guardianship.

5. The relationship of the minor to any identified prospective guardian, the duration and nature of the relationship, the motivation for seeking guardianship, and a statement from the minor concerning the guardianship, unless the minor's age or physical, emotional, or other condition precludes the minor's meaningful response, and if so, a description of the condition.

6. An analysis of the likelihood that the minor would be adopted if parental rights were terminated.

The person responsible for preparing the assessment may be called and examined by any party to the guardianship proceeding.

At this guardianship hearing:

(B) If the court finds that the minor is a person described by Section 300, it may, without adjudicating the minor a dependent child of the court, order that services be provided to keep the family together and place the minor and the minor's parent or guardian under the supervision of the probation officer for a time period consistent with Section 301.

(C) If the family subsequently is unable or unwilling to cooperate with the services being provided, the probation officer may file a petition with the juvenile court pursuant to Section 332 alleging that a previous petition has been sustained and that disposition pursuant to subdivision (b) has been ineffective in ameliorating the situation requiring the child welfare services. Upon hearing the petition, the court shall order either that the petition shall be dismissed or that a new disposition hearing shall be held pursuant to subdivision (d).

(D) If the court finds that the minor is a person described by Section 300, it may order and adjudge the minor to be a dependent child of the court.

WELFARE AND INSTITUTIONS CODE SECTION 388
PETITION TO MODIFY ORDER OR
TO TERMINATE JURISDICTION

A parent or other person having an interest in a child who is a dependent child of the juvenile court or the child himself through a properly appointed guardian may, upon grounds of change of circumstance or new evidence, petition the court in the same action in which the child was found to be a dependent child of the juvenile court or in which a guardianship was ordered pursuant to Section 360 for a hearing to change, modify, or set aside any order of court previously made or to terminate the jurisdiction of the court. The petition shall be verified and, if made by a person other than the child, shall state the petitioner's relationship to, or interest in, the child and shall set forth in concise language any change of circumstance or new evidence which are alleged to require such change of order or termination of jurisdiction.

If it appears that the best interests of the child may be promoted by the proposed change of order or termination of jurisdiction, the court shall order that a hearing be held and shall give prior notice, or cause prior notice to given, to such persons and by such means as prescribed by Section 386, and, in such instances as the means of giving notice is not prescribed by such sections, then by such means as the court prescribes.

PERSONAL NOTES:

SUPERVISION OF PARENT/CHILD VISIT GUIDELINES

California Rules of Court Section 26.2
Uniform Standards of Practice for Providers of Supervised Visitation

(a) **[Scope of service]** This section defines the duties and obligations for providers of supervised visitation as set forth in Family Code section 3200. Unless specified otherwise, the standards are designed to apply to all providers of supervised visitation, whether the provider is a friend, relative, paid independent contractor, an employee, intern or volunteer operating independently or through a supervised visitation center or agency. The goal of these standards is to assure the safety and welfare of the child, adults, and providers of supervised visitation. Once safety is assured, the best interest of the child is the paramount consideration at all stages and particularly in deciding the manner in which supervision is provided. Each court is encouraged to adopt local court rules necessary to implement these standards.

(b) **(Definition)** Family Code Section 3200 defines a provider as any individual or any supervised visitation center who monitors visitation. Supervised visitation is contact between a noncustodial party and one or more children in the presence of a neutral third person. These standards and this definition are not applicable to supervision of visitation exchanges only, but may be useful in that context.

(c) **[Qualifications, experience, and training of the provider]** Who provides the supervision and the manner in which supervision is provided depends on different factors including local resources, the financial situation of the parties, and the degree of risk in each case. While the court makes the final decision as to the manner in which supervision is provided and any terms or conditions, the court may consider recommendations by the attorney for the child, the parties and their attorneys, Family Court Services and staff, evaluators, therapists, and providers of supervised visitation. There are three kinds of providers: nonprofessional, professional, and therapeutic. The minimum qualifications for providers are

as follows:

(1) The nonprofessional provider is any person who is not paid for providing supervised visitation services. Unless otherwise ordered by the court or stipulated by the parties, the nonprofessional provider should: (i) be 21 years of age or older; (ii) have no conviction for driving under the influence (DUI) within the last 5 years; (iii) not have been on probation or parole for the last 10 years; (iv) have no record of conviction for child molestation, child abuse, or other crimes against a person; (v) have proof of automobile insurance if transporting the child; (vi) have no civil, criminal, or juvenile restraining orders within the last 10 years; (vii) have no current or past court order in which the provider is the person being supervised; (viii) not be financially dependent upon the person being supervised; (ix) have no conflict of interest as per subdivision (f) of this section; and (x) agree to adhere to and enforce the court order regarding supervised visitation.

(2) The professional provider is any person paid for providing supervised visitation services, or an independent contractor, employee, intern, or volunteer operating independently or through a supervised visitation center or agency. The professional and therapeutic provider should: (i) be 21 years of age or older; (ii) have no conviction for driving under the influence (DUI) within the last 5 years; (iii) not have been on probation or parole for the last 10 years; (iv) have no record of a conviction for child molestation, child abuse, or other crimes against a person; (v) have proof of automobile insurance if transporting the child; (vi) have no civil, criminal, or juvenile restraining orders within the last 10 years; (vii) have no current or past court order in which the provider is the person being supervised; (viii) be able to speak the language of the party supervised and of the child, or provide a neutral interpreter over the

age of 18; (ix) have no conflict of interest as per subdivision (f) of this section; and (x) agree to adhere to and enforce the court order regarding supervised visitation.

(3) The therapeutic provider is a licensed mental health professional paid for providing supervised visitation services, including but not limited to the following: a psychiatrist, psychologist, clinical social worker, marriage and family counselor, or intern working under direct supervision. A judicial officer may order a therapeutic supervision for cases requiring a clinical setting.

(4) Each court is encouraged to make available to all providers informational materials about the role of the provider, the terms and conditions of supervised visitation as per subdivision (i) of this section, and the legal responsibilities and obligations of a provider as per subdivisions (k) and (I) of this section. In addition, the professional and therapeutic providers of supervised visitation should receive training including but not limited to the following: (i) the role of a professional and therapeutic provider; (ii) child abuse reporting laws; (iii) record-keeping procedures; (iv) screening, monitoring, and termination of visitation; (v) developmental needs for children; (vi) legal responsibilities and obligations of a provider; (vii) cultural sensitivity; (viii) conflicts of interest; (ix) confidentiality; and (x) issues relating to substance abuse, child abuse, sexual abuse, and domestic violence.

(d) **[Safety and security procedures]** All providers should make every reasonable effort to assure the safety and welfare of the child and adults during the visitation. Supervised visitation centers should establish a written protocol with the assistance of the local law enforcement agency that describes what emergency assistance and responses can be expected from the local police or sheriff's department. In addition, the professional and therapeutic provider should do all of the following:

(1) Establish and set forth in writing minimum security procedures and inform the parties of

these procedures prior to the commencement of supervised visitation;

(2) Conduct a comprehensive intake and screening to assess the nature and degree of risk for each case. The procedures for intake should include separate interviews with the parties before the first visit. During the interview, the provider should obtain identifying information and explain the reasons for temporary suspension or termination of a visit as specified in subdivision (m) of this section. If the child is of sufficient age and capacity, the provider should include him or her in part of the intake or orientation process. Any discussion should be presented to the child in a manner appropriate to the child's developmental stage;

(3) Obtain during the intake process, (i) copies of any protective order, (ii) current court orders, (iii) any Judicial Council form relating to supervised visitation orders, (iv) a report of any written records of allegations of domestic violence or abuse, and (v) in the case of a child's chronic health condition, an account of his or her health needs;

(4) Establish written procedures to follow in the event a child is abducted during supervised visitation; and

(5) Suspend or terminate supervised visitation if the provider determines that the risk factors present are placing in jeopardy the safety and welfare of the child or provider as enumerated in subdivision (i) of this section.

(c) **[Ratio of children to provider]** The ratio of children to professional provider should be contingent upon:

(1) The degree of risk factors present in each case;

(2) The nature of supervision required in each case;

(3) The number and ages of the children to be supervised during a visit;

(4) The number of people visiting the child during the visit;

(5) The duration and location of the visit; and

(6) The experience of the provider.

(f) **[Conflict of Interest]** All providers should maintain a neutral role by refusing to discuss the merits of the case, or agree with or support one party over another.   Any discussion between a provider and the parties should be for the purposes of arranging visitation and providing for the safety of the children. In order to avoid a conflict of interest, no provider should:

(1) Be financially dependent on the person being supervised;

(2) Be an employee of the person being supervised;

(3) Be an employee of or affiliated with any superior or municipal court in the county in which the supervision is ordered unless specified in the employment contract; or

(4) Be in an intimate relationship with the person being supervised.

(g) **[Maintenance and disclosure of records]** The professional and therapeutic provider should keep a record for each case, including but not limited to the following: (i) a written record of each contact and visit including the date, time and duration of the contact or visit; (ii) who attended the visit; (iii) a summary of activities during the visit; (iv) actions taken by the provider, including any interruptions, termination of a visit, and reasons for these actions; (v) an account of critical incidents, including physical or verbal alterations and threats; (vi) violations of protective or court visitation orders; (vii) any failure to comply with the terms and conditions of the visitation as per subdivision (i) of this section; and (viii) any incidence of abuse as required by law.

(1) Case recordings should be limited to facts, observations, and direct statements made by the parties, not personal conclusions, suggestions, or opinions of the provider. All contacts by the provider in person, in writing, or by telephone with either party, the children, the court,

attorneys, mental health professionals, and referring agencies, should be documented in the case file. All entries should be dated and signed by the person recording the entry.

(2) If ordered by the court, or requested by either party or the attorney for the child, a report about the supervised visit should be produced. These reports should include facts, observations, and direct statements and not opinions or recommendations regarding future visitation unless ordered by the court.

A copy of any report should be sent to all parties, and the attorney for the child.

(3) Any identifying information about the parties and the child, including addresses, telephone numbers, places of employment, and schools, is confidential, should not be disclosed, and should be deleted from documents before releasing them to any court, attorney, attorney for the child, party, mediator, evaluator, mental health professional, social worker, or referring agency, except as required in reporting suspected child abuse.

(h) **[Confidentiality]**   Communications between parties and providers of supervised visitation are not protected by any privilege of confidentiality.   The psychotherapist-patient privilege does not apply during therapeutic supervision.

The professional and therapeutic provider should, whenever possible, maintain confidentiality regarding the case except when (i) ordered by the court; (ii) subpoenaed to produce records or testify in court; (iii) requested by a mediator or evaluator in conjunction with a court-ordered mediation, investigation, or evaluation; (iv) required by Child Protective Services; or (v) requested by law enforcement.

(i) **[Delineation of terms and conditions]** The sole responsibility for enforcement of all the terms and conditions of any supervised visitation is the provider's. The terms and conditions for any supervised visitation, unless otherwise ordered by the court, are as follows:

(1) Monitor conditions to assure the safety and welfare of the child;

(2) Enforce the frequency and duration of the visits as ordered by the court;

(3) Avoid any attempt to take sides with either party;

(4) Ensure that all contact between the child and the noncustodial party is within the provider's hearing and sight at all times and that discussions are audible to the provider, unless a different order is issued by the court;

(5) Speak in a language spoken by the child and noncustodial party;

(6) Allow no derogatory comments about the other parent, his or her family, caretaker, child, or child's siblings;

(7) Allow no discussion of the court case or possible future outcomes;

(8) Allow no provider nor the child to be used to gather information about the other party or caretaker or to transmit documents, information, or personal possessions;

(9) Allow no spanking, hitting, or threatening the child;

(10) Allow no visits to occur while the visiting party appears to be under the influence of alcohol or illegal drugs;

(11) Allow no emotional, verbal, physical, or sexual abuse; and

(12) Ensure that the parties follow any additional rules established by the provider or the court.

(j) **[Safety considerations for sexual abuse cases]** In cases where there are allegations of sexual abuse, the following additional terms and conditions are applicable to all providers, unless authorized by the court:

(1) Allow no exchanges of gifts, money, or cards;

(2) Allow no photographing, audio taping, or videotaping of the children;

(3) Allow no physical contact such as lap sitting, hair combing, stroking, hand holding, prolonged hugging, wrestling, tickling, horseplaying, changing diapers, or accompanying the child to the bathroom;

(4) Allow no whispering, passing notes, hand signals, or body signals; and

(5) Allow no supervised visitation in the location where the alleged sexual abuse occurred.

(k) **[Legal responsibilities and obligations of a provider]** All providers of supervised visitation have the following responsibilities:

(1) Advise the parties before commencement of supervised visitation that no confidential privilege exists;

(2) Report suspected child abuse to the appropriate agency, as provided by law, and inform the parties of the provider's obligation to make such reports;

(3) Implement the terms and conditions as per subdivision (i) of this section; and

(4) Suspend or terminate visitation as per subdivision (m) of this section.

(l) **[Additional legal responsibilities for professional and therapeutic providers]** In addition to the preceding legal responsibilities and obligations, the professional and therapeutic provider should:

(1) Prepare a written contract to be signed by the parents before commencement of the supervised visitation. The contract should inform each party of the terms and conditions of supervised visitation;

(2) Review custody and visitation orders relevant to supervised visitation;

(3) Implement an intake and screening procedure as per subdivision (d) (2) of this

section; and

(4) Comply with additional requirements as per subdivision (n) of this section.

(m) **[Temporary suspension or termination of supervised visitation]** All providers should make every reasonable effort to provide a safe visit for the child and the noncustodial party. However, if a provider determines that the rules of the visit have been violated, the child has become acutely distressed, or the safety of the child or the provider is at risk, the visit may be temporarily interrupted, rescheduled at a later date, or terminated. All interruptions or terminations of visits should be recorded in the case file.

All providers should advise both parties of the reasons for interruption of a visit or termination.

(n) **[Additional requirements for professional and therapeutic providers]** The professional and therapeutic provider should also state the reasons for temporary suspension or termination of supervised visitation in writing and provide them to both parties, their attorneys, the attorney for the child, and the court.

PENAL CODE SUPERVISION OF PARENT/CHILD VISIT GUIDELINES

Supervised visits are often ordered by the court so the child can have a continuing relationship with a parent. The job of a supervisor is to guarantee the welfare of the child. The supervisor should maintain a neutral attitude toward the Mother, the Father, and/or the Guardian, and any bias shall be only for the child's well being.

To that end, the supervisor shall ensure that:

(1) The child is free to have an enjoyable experience with the supervised person.

(2) The child is physically safe.

(3) The child is not exposed to behaviors that would be unduly stressful and emotionally upsetting.

(4) The supervisor can verify that the supervised person was or was not appropriate, and persons not present will not have to rely on interpretations of what the child reports at a later time.

Certain behaviors are necessary to assure that these objectives can be met. These behaviors are based on valid psychological principles which are directed primarily toward the welfare of the child yet also addresses the feelings and concerns of the parents.

   (a)   The supervised person is not to be alone with the child or engage in whispered conversations.

   (b)   The supervised person can invite, but not demand, or coerce, physical contact with the child.

   (c)   Gifts or other visitors may be very stressful by virtue of their unexpectedness an/or inappropriateness. Prior approval of the supervisor must be obtained.

   (d)   Because past events may have caused stress/trauma and the child is uncertain about the future, references to past events and future plans should be avoided in discussions with the child. The visit should focus on the present so that the child experiences a calm and pleasurable visit.

If the behavior of the supervised person does not conform to this guideline or in any other way, jeopardizes the physical or emotional well-being of the child, the visit will be terminated.

If there is any suspicion that the supervised person's behavior was abusive, you are encouraged to report those suspicions to the law enforcement agency in which the visit occurred (city police or county sheriff) or the appropriate Child Protective Services Agency.

SUPERVISORS WHO RECEIVE FINANCIAL COMPENSATION

California Penal Code section 11165 requires that for any person who receives financial compensation for monitoring a court-ordered visit between a child and any other person that person shall be trained in the mandatory reporting requirements listed in that Penal Code section.   The mediator/trainer will provide a copy for you to read, and will review the Penal Code with you after you have read it.

PENAL CODE SECTION 11165.15 CHILD VISITATION MONITOR
As used in this article, child visitation "monitor" means any person who, for financial compensation, acts as a monitor of a visit between a child and any other person when the monitoring of that visit has been ordered by a court of law.

PENAL CODE SECTION 11166 DUTY TO REPORT
(a)   Except as provided in subdivision (b), any child care custodian, health practitioner, employee of a child protective agency, child visitation monitor, fire fighter, animal control officer, or humane society officer who has knowledge of or observes a child in professional capacity or within the scope of his or her employment whom he or she knows or reasonably suspects has been the victim of child abuse shall report the known or suspected instance of child abuse to a child protective agency immediately or as soon as practically possible by telephone and shall prepare and send a written report thereof within 36 hours of receiving the information concerning the incident.   A child protective agency shall be notified and a report shall be prepared and sent even if the child has expired, regardless of whether or not the possible abuse was a factor contributing to the death, and even if suspected child abuse was discovered during an autopsy.

For the purposes of this article, "reasonable suspicion" means that it is objectively reasonable for a person to entertain such a suspicion, based upon facts that could cause a reasonable person in a like position, drawing when appropriate on his or her training and experience, to suspect child abuse.   For the purpose of this article, the pregnancy of a minor does not, in and of itself, constitute the basis of reasonable suspicion of sexual abuse.

(b)   Any child care custodian, health practitioner, employee of a child protective agency, child visitation monitor, fire fighter, animal control officer, or humane society officer who has knowledge of or who reasonably suspects that mental suffering has been inflicted upon a child or that his or her emotional well-being is endangered in any other way, may report the known or suspected instance of child abuse to a child protective agency.

(c)   (1) Except as provided in paragraph (2) and subdivision (d), any clergy member who has knowledge of or observes a child in his or her professional capacity or in the scope of his or her duties, whom he or she knows or reasonably suspects has been the victim of child abuse, shall report the known or suspected instance of child abuse to a child protective agency immediately   or   as   soon   as practically possible by telephone and shall prepare and send a written report thereof within

36 hours of receiving the information concerning the incident. A child protective agency shall be notified and a report shall be prepared and sent even if the child has expired, regardless of whether or not the possible abuse was a factor contributing to the death. (2) A clergy member who acquires knowledge or reasonable suspicion of child abuse during a penitential communication is not subject to paragraph (1). For the purpose of this subdivision, "penitential communication" means a communication, intended to be in confidence, including, but not limited to, a sacramental confession, made to a clergy member who, in the course of the discipline or practice of his or her church, denomination, or organization, is authorized or accustomed to hear those communications, and under the discipline, tenets, customs, or practices of his or her church, denomination, or organization, has a duty to keep those communications secret. (3) Nothing in this subdivision shall be construed to modify or limit a clergy member's duty to report known or suspected child abuse when he or she is acting in the capacity as a child care custodian, health practitioner, employee of the child protective agency, child visitation monitor, fire fighter, animal control officer, humane society officer, or commercial film print processor.

(d)   Any member of the clergy who has knowledge of or who reasonably suspects that mental suffering has been inflicted upon a child or that his or her emotional well-being is endangered in any other way may report the known or suspected instance of child abuse to a child protective agency.

(e)   Any commercial film and photographic print processor who has knowledge of, or observes, within the scope of his or her professional capacity or employment, any film, photograph, videotape, negative or slide depicting a child under the age of 16 years engaged in an act of sexual conduct, shall report the instance of suspected child abuse to the law enforcement agency having jurisdiction over the case immediately, or as soon as practically possible, by telephone and shall prepare and send a written report of it with a copy of the film, photograph, videotape, negative or slide attached within 36 hours of receiving the information concerning the incident. As used in this subdivision, "sexual conduct" means any of the following:

(1)   Sexual intercourse, including genital-genital, oral-genital, anal-genital, or oral-anal, whether between persons of the same or opposite sex or between humans and animals.

(2)   Penetration of the vagina or rectum by any object.

(3)   Masturbation for the purpose of sexual stimulation of the viewer.

(4)   Sadomasochistic abuse for the purpose of sexual stimulation of the viewer.

(5)   Exhibition of the genitals, pubic, or rectal areas of any person for the purpose of sexual stimulation of the viewer.

(f)   Any other person who has knowledge of, or observes, a child whom he or she knows or reasonably suspects has been a victim of child abuse may report the known or suspected instance of child abuse to a child protective agency.

(g)   When two or more persons who are required to report are present and jointly have knowledge of a known or suspected instance of child abuse, and when there is agreement among them, the telephone report may be made by a member of the team selected by mutual agreement and a single report may be made and signed by the selected member of the reporting team. Any member who has knowledge that the member designated to report has failed to do so shall thereafter make the report.

(h)   The reporting duties under this section are individual, and no supervisor or administrator may impede or prohibit the reporting duties, and no person making a report shall be subject to any sanction for making the report. However, internal procedures to facilitate reporting and apprise supervisors and administrators of reports may be established provided that they are not inconsistent with this article. The internal procedures shall not require any employee required to make reports pursuant to this article to disclose his or her identity to the employer.

(i)   A county probation or welfare department shall immediately, or as soon as practically possible, report by telephone to the law enforcement agency having jurisdiction over the case, to the agency given the responsibility for investigation for cases under

Section 300 of the Welfare and Institutions Code, and to the District Attorney's office every known or suspected instance of child abuse, as defined in section 11165.6 except acts or omissions coming within (b) of section 11165.2, or reports made pursuant to section 11165.13 based on risks to a child which relate solely to the inability of the parent to provide the child with regular care due to the parents' substance abuse which shall be reported only to the county welfare department. A county probation or welfare department also shall send a written report thereof within 36 hours of receiving the information concerning the incident to any agency to which it is required to make a telephone report under this subdivision.

A law enforcement agency shall immediately or as soon as practically possible, report by telephone to the agency given responsibility for investigation of cases under Section 300 of the Welfare and Institutions Code and to the district attorney's office every known or suspected instance of child abuse reported to it, except acts or omissions coming within subdivision (d) of Section 11165.2, which shall be reported only to the county welfare department. A law enforcement agency shall report to the county welfare department every known or suspected instance of child abuse reported to it which is alleged to have occurred as a result of the action of a person responsible for a child's welfare, or as a result of the failure of a person responsible for the child's welfare to adequately protect the minor from abuse where the person responsible for the child's welfare knew or reasonably should have known that the minor was in danger of abuse. A law enforcement also shall send a written report thereof within 36 hours of receiving the information concerning the incident to any agency to which it is required to make a telephone report under this subdivision.

PENAL CODE SECTION 11166.5 STATEMENT ACKNOWLEDGING AWARENESS OF REPORTING DUTIES AND PROMISING COMPLIANCE; EXEMPTIONS; DISTRIBUTION IN CONNECTION WITH LICENSURE OR CERTIFICATION.
(a) On and after January 1, 1985, any person who enters into employment as a child care custodian, health practitioner, fire fighter, animal control officer, or humane society officer, or with a child protective agency, prior to commencing his or her employment, and as a prerequisite to that employment, shall sign a statement on a form provided to him or her by his or her employer to the effect that he or she has knowledge of the provision of Section 11166 and will comply with those provisions.

On and after January 1, 1993, any person who acts as a child visitation monitor, as defined in Section 11165.15, prior to engaging in monitoring the first visit in a case, shall sign a statement in a form provided to him or her by the court which ordered the presence of that third person during the visit, to the effect that he or she has knowledge of the provisions of Section 11166 and will comply with those provisions.

The statement shall include all of the following provisions:
Section 11166 of the Penal code requires any child care custodian, health practitioner, fire fighter, animal control officer, or humane society officer, employee of a child protective agency, or child visitation monitor who has knowledge of, or observes, a child in his or her professional capacity or within the scope of his or her employment whom he or she knows or reasonably suspects has been the victim of child abuse to report the known or suspected instance of child abuse to a child protective agency immediately, or as soon as practically possible, by telephone and to prepare and send a written report thereof within 36 hours of receiving the information concerning the incident.
"Child care custodian" includes teacher; an instructional aide, a teacher's aide, or a teacher's assistant employed by any public or private school, who has been trained in the duties imposed by this article, if the school district has so warranted to the State Department of Education; a classified employee of any public school who has been trained in the duties imposed by this article, if the school has so warranted to the State Department of Education; administrative officers, supervisors of child welfare and attendance, or certificated pupil personnel employees of any public or private school; administrators of a public or

private day camp; administrators and employees of public or private youth centers, youth recreation programs, or youth organizations; administrators and employees of public or private organizations who duties require direct contact and supervision of children and who have been trained in the duties imposed by this article; licensees, administrators, and employees of licensed community care or child daycare facilities; headstart teachers; licensing workers or licensing evaluators; public assistance workers; employees of a child care institution including, but not limited to, foster parents, group home personnel, and personnel of residential care facilities; social workers, probation officers, or parole officers; employees of a school district police or security department; any person who is an administrator or a presenter of, or a counselor in, a child abuse prevention program in any public or private school; a district attorney investigator, inspector, or family support officer unless the investigator, inspector, or office is working with an attorney appointed pursuant to Section 317 of the Welfare and Institutions Code to represent a minor; or a peace officer, as defined in Chapter 4.5 (commencing with Section 830) of Title 3 of Part 2 of this code, who is not otherwise described in this section.

"Health practitioner" includes physicians and surgeons, psychiatrist, psychologist, dentist, residents, interns, podiatrist, chiropractors, licensed nurses, dental hygienists, optometrists, or any other person who is licensed under Division 2 (commencing with Section 500) of the Business and Professions Code; marriage, family and child counselors; emergency medical technicians I or II, paramedics, or other persons certified pursuant to Division 2.5 (commencing with Section 1797) of the Health and Safety Code; psychological assistants registered pursuant to Section 2913 of the Business and Professions Code; marriage, family, and child counselor trainees as defined in subdivision (c) of Section 4980.03 of the Business and Professions Code; unlicensed marriage, family and child counselor interns registered under Section 4980.44 of the Business and Professions Code; state or county public health employees who treat minors for venereal disease or any other condition;

coroners; paramedics; and religious practitioners who diagnose, examine, or treat minors for venereal disease or any other condition; coroners; and paramedics.

"Child visitation monitor" means any person as defined in Section 11165.15.

The signed statements shall be retained by the employer or the court, as the case may be. The cost of printing, distribution, and filing of these statements shall be borne by the employer or the court.

This subdivision is not applicable to persons employed by child protective agencies, public or private youth centers, youth recreation programs, and youth organizations as members of the support staff or maintenance staff and who do not work with, observe, or have knowledge of children as part of their official duties.

(b)   On and after January 1, 1986, when a person is issued a state license or certificate to engage in a profession or occupation, the members of which are required to make a report pursuant to Section 11166, the state agency issuing the license or certificate shall send a statement substantially similar to the one contained in subdivision (a), the statement also shall indicate that failure to comply with the requirements of Section 11166 is a misdemeanor, punishable by up to six months in a county jail, by a fine of one thousand dollars ($1,000), or by both that imprisonment and fine.

(c)   As an alternative to the procedure required by subdivision (b), a state agency may cause the required statement to be printed on all application forms for a license or certificate printed on or before January 1, 1986.

(d)   On or after January 1, 1993, any child visitation monitor, as defined in Section 11165.15, who desires to act in that capacity shall have received training in the duties imposed by this article, including training in child abuse identification and child abuse reporting. The person, prior to engaging in monitoring the first visit in a case, shall sign a statement on a form provided to him or her by the court which ordered the presence of the third person during the visit, to the effect that he or she has received this training. This statement may be included in the statement required by subdivision (a) or it may be a separate statement. This statement shall be filed, along with the statement required by subdivision (a), in the court file of the case for which the visitation monitoring is being provided.

PENAL CODE SECTION 11167.
REQUIRED INFORMATION;
CONFIDENTIALITY OF REPORTER'S
IDENTITY
(a)   A telephone report of a known or suspected instance of child abuse shall include the name of the person making the report, the name of the child, the present location of the child, the nature and extent of the injury, and any other information, including information that led that person to suspect child abuse, requested by the child protective agency.
(b)   Information relevant to the incident of child abuse may also be given to an investigator from a child protective agency who is investigating the known or suspected case of child abuse.
(c)   Information relevant to the incident of child abuse may be given to the licensing agency when it is investigating a known or suspected case of child abuse, including the investigation report, and other pertinent materials.
(d)   The identity of all persons who report under this article shall be confidential and disclosed only between child protective agency, or to counsel representing a child protective agency, or to the district attorney in a criminal prosecution or in an action initiated under Section 602 of the Welfare and Institutions Code arising from alleged child abuse, or to counsel appointed pursuant to subdivision (c) of Section 317 of the Welfare and Institutions Code, or to the county counsel or district attorney in a proceeding under Part 4 (commencing with Section 7800) of Division 12 of the Family Code or Section 300 of the Welfare and Institutions Code, or to a licensing agency when abuse in out-of-home care is reasonable suspected, or when those persons waive confidentiality, or by court order.
(e)   Persons who may report pursuant to subdivision (d) of Section 11166 are not required to include their names.

PENAL CODE SECTION 1167.5
CONFIDENTIALITY AND DISCLOSURE
OF REPORTS; PUNISHMENT FOR THE
VIOLATION OF CONFIDENTIALITY
(a)   The reports required by Sections 11166 and 11166.2 shall be confidential and may be disclosed only as provided in subdivision (b). Any violation of the confidentiality provided by this article shall be a misdemeanor punishable by up to six months in jail or by a fine of five hundred dollars ($500) or by both.
(b)   Reports of suspected child abuse and information contained therein may be disclosed only to the following:
(1)   Persons or agencies to whom disclosure of the identity of the reporting party is permitted under Section 11167.
(2)   Persons or agencies to whom disclosure of information is permitted under subdivision (b) of Section 11170.
(3)   Persons or agencies with whom investigations of child abuse are coordinated under the regulations promulgated under Section 11174.
(4)   Multidisciplinary personnel teams as defined in subdivision (d) of Section 18951 of the Welfare and Institutions Code.
(5)   Persons or agencies responsible for the licensing of facilities which care for children, as specified in Section 11165.7
(6)   The State Department of Social Services or any county licensing agency which has contracted with the state, as specified in paragraph (3) of subdivision (b) of Section 11170, when an individual has applied for a community care license or child day care license, or for employment in an out-of-home care facility, or when a complaint alleges child abuse by an operator or employee of an out-of-home care facility.
(7) Hospital scan teams. As used in this paragraph, "hospital scan team" means a team of three or more persons established by a hospital, or two or more hospitals in the same county, consisting of health care professionals and representatives of law enforcement and child protective services, the members of which are engaged in the identification of child abuse. The disclosure authorized by this section includes disclosure among hospital scan teams

located in the same county.

(8)   Coroners and medical examiners when conducting a post mortem examination of a child.

(9)   The Board of Prison Terms may subpoena reports that (A) are not unfounded, pursuant to Section 11165.12, and (B) concern only the current incidents upon which parole revocation proceedings are pending against a parolee charged with child abuse. The reports and information shall be confidential pursuant to subdivision (d) of Section 11167.

(c)   Authorized persons within county health departments shall be permitted to receive copies of any reports made by health practitioners, as defined in Section 11155.8, pursuant to Section 11165.13, and copies of assessments completed pursuant to Sections 10900 and 10901 of the Health and Safety code, to the extent permitted by federal law. Any information received pursuant to this subdivision is protected by subdivision (e).

(d)   Nothing in this section shall be interpreted to require the Department of Justice to disclose information contained in records maintained under Section 11169 or under the regulations promulgated pursuant to Section 11174, except as otherwise provided in this article.

(e)   This section shall not be interpreted to allow disclosure of any reports or records relevant to the reports of child abuse if the disclosure would be prohibited by any other provisions of state or federal law applicable to the reports or records relevant to the reports of child abuse.

LEGAL ACKNOWLEDGMENTS

_____   I acknowledge that I have read and understand this
                 document;
_____   I have reviewed California Penal Code sections
                 11165.15 and 11166.5; and
_____   I understand that I must report any suspected child
                 abuse that may occur during the period I am monitoring a visit.

_____   _____
(Signature)   (Print Your Name)

_____   _____
(Date of Training)   (Name of Court Case)

_____
(Case Number)

FEDERAL LAW REGARDING SCHOOL RECORDS

Family Education Rights and Privacy Act - FERPA

Generally, a school is not required to provide parents with copies of records. However, if the distance is great enough to make it impractical for the parent to visit the school to review the records, the school must make copies of the records and send them to the parent. (The school may charge a reasonable fee for copying and also include the cost of mailing).

The FERPA does not address conferences for the purpose of disclosing student performance. Thus, a school has no obligation under this law to arrange a conference to accommodate the non-custodial parent. However, if records of conferences are maintained, the non-custodial parent has the right to see those records.

The school is not required to provide the non-custodial parent with general notices about lunch menus, PTA information, or announcements of teacher conferences since these are not "education records" under FERPA definition.

The FERPA does not require a school to honor a standing request, but the school may do so if it wishes. If parents wish to obtain information from their child's records on a regular basis, they should submit request periodically. The school must respond to each request within forty-five (45) days.

Any parent may ask the school for the opportunity to review records, either by going to where the records are kept or by requesting copies. The school may ask the parent for some identification.

The parent with custody may not prevent the non-custodian parent from exercising his or her rights, or is permission needed from the custodial parent to provide access to school records.

The act specifically requires that in the case of divorce or separation, a school district must provide access to records to both natural parents, custodial and non-custodial, unless there is a legally binding document that specifically removes that parent's right to access. In this context, a legally binding document is a court order or other legal paper that prohibits access to education records, or removes the parent's right to have knowledge about his or her child's education.

PERSONAL NOTES:

PERSONAL NOTES: